THE
OCEAN
BOOK

by Frank Sherwin

THE OCEAN BOOK

First Printing: May 2004
Second Printing: April 2006
Third Printing: July 2008

Printed in China

Cover and Interior Design by Bryan Miller
Illustrations by Bryan Miller
Contributing editors: Debbie Brooks and Beth Wiles

For information write:
Master Books
P.O. Box 726
Green Forest, AR 72638

Please visit our website for other great titles:
www.masterbooks.net

ISBN-13: 978-0-89051-401-6
ISBN-10: 0-89051-401-1
Library of Congress number: 2003116033

Wonders of Creation Series

The Astronomy Book	978-0-89051-250-0	
Jonathan Henry	$15.99 • Case • 80 pages	
The Cave Book	978-0-89051-496-2	
Emil Silvestru	$15.99 • Case • 80 pages	
The Fossil Book	978-0-89051-438-2	
Dr. Gary Parker	$15.99 • Case • 80 pages	
The Geology Book	978-0-89051-281-4	
John D. Morris	$15.99 • Case • 80 pages	
The Weather Book	978-0-89051-211-1	
Michael Oard	$15.99 • Case • 80 pages	

Dedication:
To my first mate Jan and our swabbies
JoHannah, Marya, Llynea, and Roy

Table of Contents

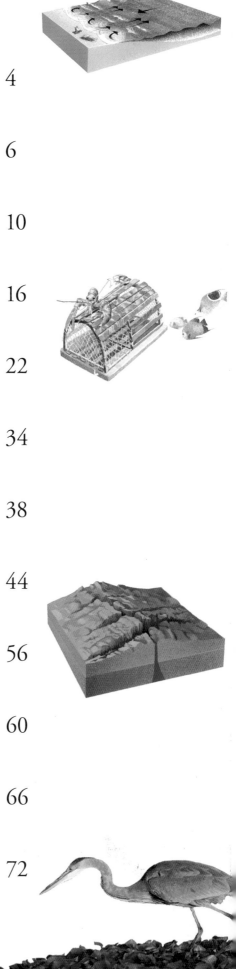

INTRODUCTION

A snapshot of Earth from space reveals its nickname, the "Blue Planet." With water covering 71 percent of its total surface area, Earth does indeed appear blue to any space traveler. Most of this blue coloring comes from Earth's oceans, which contain 97 percent of all the surface water on the planet. Filling an average depth of 2½ miles, Earth's oceans would cover the surface of her moon *nine times*!

Where did all the water come from? How were the oceans formed? Scripture tells us, "In the beginning God created the heaven and the earth" (Genesis 1:1). In the thirty verses to follow, the word *water* appears ten times. The apostle Peter also describes creation as "the earth standing out of the water and in the water" (2 Peter 3:5). The biblical account explains that God gathered these waters into seas and filled them with life. This was done for His pleasure and for our use. Water is a precious, essential gift from the Creator. As faithful stewards of the earth's resources, it is important that mankind understand the seas He created, so that they can take good care of them and everything in them.

If you are a landlubber nearing the shore for the first time, you will probably hear the ocean's thundering power before you see its vast blue expanse. Perhaps you will view it from a lofty Pacific cliff, or as you trudge through Atlantic sands to the crashing surf. Welcome to the fascinating study of the world's oceans — with all their beauty, power, flora, and fauna.

The oceans can be thought of as *protective*, like a blanket that Almighty God has cast over the surface of the earth. Along with the atmosphere, the oceans help to regulate the climate and weather of the world. Because water is so effective in absorbing heat, the oceans act as heat reservoirs that moderate the cold of winter and the heat of summer. The oceans are also *provisional*, directly providing food for sustenance and life-giving oxygen released from tiny, free-floating photosynthetic organisms. Most people know that plants supply the atmosphere with oxygen; what they do not know is that plants contribute only half of the oxygen. Those tiny ocean organisms produce the other half. Indirectly,

OTHER WORLD SEAS

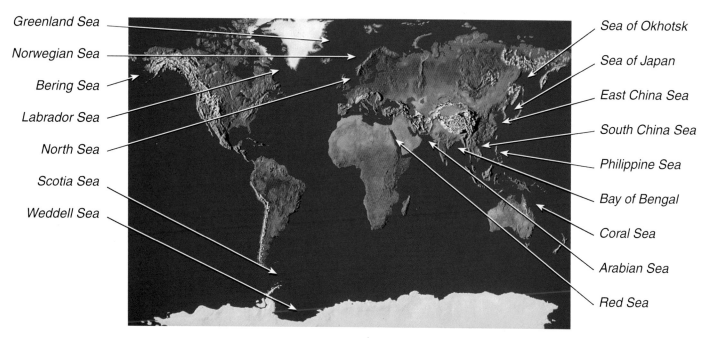

Greenland Sea
Norwegian Sea
Bering Sea
Labrador Sea
North Sea
Scotia Sea
Weddell Sea

Sea of Okhotsk
Sea of Japan
East China Sea
South China Sea
Philippine Sea
Bay of Bengal
Coral Sea
Arabian Sea
Red Sea

the oceans provide precipitation by acting as the source of rain for crops. Heavy ocean breakers, tides and currents also reveal that our oceans are *powerful*, a source of almost limitless energy for man's potential use.

Human history is closely connected to the oceans. Centuries ago, the Gulf of Mexico, the Caribbean and Mediterranean Seas, and the Indian, Pacific, Atlantic and Arctic Oceans were referred to by some as the "seven seas" or those bodies of water that were navigable. As exploration continued through the decades, oceanographers saw the Gulf of Mexico, the Caribbean Sea, and the Mediterranean Sea as marginal seas of the Atlantic Ocean. They also distinguished the Antarctic Ocean from those oceans to its north. Today these vast bodies of water serve as a great liquid highway for commercial ships, act as borders between nations, supply one-third of usable natural gas and petroleum, and provide a major source of a variety of foods and recreation. God's creative hand is clearly seen in preparing this planet with its life-supporting oceans for our habitation.

The oceans contain the greatest number of living things on Earth. Many of the most amazing creatures in God's creation reside in the salty deep. Incredibly beautiful life forms inhabit the sparkling, sunlit waters of areas such as Australia's Great Barrier Reef.

God has given our planet such splendor, and our oceans are no different. People find the beautiful blue, green, and turquoise colors of the oceans to be captivating. What causes a change in the water's color? Water molecules scatter rays of sunlight as they enter the ocean. Most of the colors, except for the blue color,

are absorbed or "soaked up." The blue wavelength, or color, is reflected back to your eyes and you see a blue ocean. Something as simple as clouds passing across the sun changes the ocean's color. Tiny yellowish creatures called phytoplankton live in oceans throughout the world. The combination of their yellow color with the ocean blue gives the waters of the world different shades from yellow to blue-green. Sediment particles washed into the ocean from rivers or stirred up from the ocean floor also affect the ocean's color. Greenish-looking water can be due to phytoplankton mixed with tiny yellow-brown clay particles. When their colors combine with blue, a greenish color results. How do you suppose the Yellow Sea off the coast of China got its name?

Although three-quarters of the American population live within fifty miles of a coast, much about the oceans still remains a mystery. Scientists probably know more about the surface of the distant moon than the ocean bottom, cloaked in frigid darkness and crushing pressure. Truly, the mighty oceans with their mysterious deeps remain a vast and fascinating frontier.

"FOR THE INVISIBLE THINGS OF HIM FROM THE CREATION OF THE WORLD ARE CLEARLY SEEN, BEING UNDERSTOOD BY THE THINGS THAT ARE MADE, EVEN HIS ETERNAL POWER AND GODHEAD; SO THAT THEY ARE WITHOUT EXCUSE."
— ROMANS 1:20

Chapter One

RESEARCH AND THE DEEP OCEANS

Oceanography is the exploration and scientific study of phenomena associated with the world's seas, oceans, and their surrounding environment. This study involves such diverse fields as zoology, physics, meteorology, geography, geology and chemistry. (A student who would like to be an oceanographer must be good in math and chemistry.)

BRANCHES OF OCEANOGRAPHY

- CHEMICAL OCEANOGRAPHY involves the study of the chemical composition of seawater and material in suspension, the nature of dissolved gases and solids, chemical cycles like the carbon cycle, and the acidity of seawater in relationship to the ocean bottom and the atmosphere.
- PHYSICAL OCEANOGRAPHY includes the study of the physical features of the ocean's water, such as temperature, density, waves, currents, tides, sea ice, air-sea interaction, and the ability to transmit sound and light.
- BIOLOGICAL OCEANOGRAPHY, or marine biology, is the application of the scientific method to the ocean's animal and plant life, including chemical and physical changes, food webs, the interaction of life with its surroundings, and other related factors.
- MARINE GEOLOGY AND GEOPHYSICS are the study of the nature and physics of the ocean's solid structure, including all aspects of the continental slopes and shelves and the ocean basins. A majority of what is known in regard to the geology of the oceans has only been discovered in the last half-century.
    - The marine geologist mainly studies oceanic sediments and rocks. Some common examples of marine geology are: petrology – study of the origin, composition, structure, and properties of rocks associated with the oceans; sedimentology – the study of marine sediments; and geomorphology – the study of the origin of the seafloor and its modification by dynamic processes, such as volcanism, tidal actions, earthquakes or tsunamis.
    - The marine geophysicist, using physics and math, applies the properties of magnetism, gravity, electricity, heat flow, and seismic methods to the study of the oceanic crust and mantle.

Oceanography, a relatively young discipline, is important to many different fields, such as commerce (shipping products between nations), defense (navies of various nations), engineering (construction and operation of seagoing structures and devices), communications (laying cables along the ocean bottom), safety (tracking icebergs), mineral and petroleum exploration (finding and recovering mineral deposits and oil), and meteorology (determining weather patterns). Scores of oceanographic research ships are presently monitoring events and collecting information on and below the surface of the sea. This information will contribute to a greater understanding of the oceans God created.

Today, the following divisions of oceanography are generally distinguished: chemical oceanography, physical oceanography, marine geology and geophysics, and biological oceanography. These disciplines overlap considerably, and a good oceanographer will be knowledgeable in all areas.

The first expedition devoted to oceanographic research was in December of 1872, when the HMS *Challenger* set out from England to conduct a three-and-a-half year oceanographic expedition of the ocean floor, sea life, and seawater temperature and salinity. The *Challenger* staff of six scientists traveled 68,900 miles (110,860 km). Naturalists on board

HMS Challenger

Stone weight used for sounding

used weighted lines to sound (measure the depth of) shallower parts of the ocean, mapped very small sections of the ocean floor, studied ocean currents, and discovered more than 4,400 species of animals.

One theory the scientists wanted to examine was Professor Edward Forbes's (1815-1854) claim that life below 1,800 feet (549 m) was impossible. Forbes felt that with such poor conditions as lack of light and high pressure, life surely could not exist. His claim was clearly proven wrong. Hundreds of samples were taken during the *Challenger* voyage from depths of over five miles (8,185 m) down. The scientists found a vast array of bizarre, previously undiscovered creatures. Mysterious manganese nodules, first discovered on this expedition, were described as potato-shaped nodules ranging from walnut-size to grapefruit-size." Another significant discovery made on this voyage, a rise in the middle of the Atlantic Ocean, turned out to be the first clue to the extensive mid-oceanic ridge.

Researchers have come a long way since those early days of oceanographic studies. By the 1920s, the depth and shape of the ocean bottom were being determined by echo sounders. These devices send out a strong sound pulse that bounces or reflects off of a solid object, such as the sea floor, and returns to the source where it is recorded. In 1962, the HMS *Cook* recorded one of the deepest soundings ever in the Mindanao Trench, the echo sounder registering over 7 miles (11,515 m)!

In the 1950s and 60s, technology provided tools so sophisticated that the newly developed apparatuses could even study the earth's crust below the ocean floor. There has been more exploration of the ocean bottom since 1950 than in all the rest of recorded history.

Weights used to measure ocean depths

Today, ships use a seismic profile (a picture made by sound waves) to view the composition of the ocean bottom.

Today, ships are capable of generating a seismic profile (pictures made by sound waves) to view the composition of the ocean bottom. The devices which accomplish this task work in much the same manner as the echo sounders but are more powerful and use advanced technology.

The formidable Deep Sea Drilling Project (DSDP) was conducted from 1968 to 1983 by an international group of oceanographic institutions. Cores — thirty-foot (9.5 m) vertical, cylindrical columns of sediment and rock — were taken from the seafloor by a 400-foot long drilling ship. After core samples were extracted from the ocean bottom, scientists sometimes placed sensors into the hole to gather more information such as temperature readings. Scientists examined, and continue to examine, the composition of the thin multicolored bands of core sediments. Many thousands of core samples from various oceanic expeditions are stored in cold, hermetically sealed (airtight) rooms throughout the world. They remain, much like books in a library, available for further investigation when necessary.

In the mid-90s, the main emphasis of oceanography was exploration. Certainly, a large amount was accomplished by traditional methods using ships, but Earth-orbiting satellites were increasingly used in a method that came to be known as satellite oceanography. Now, in the 21st century, oceanographers use everything from deep sea robots to these more sophisticated satellite images to further the fascinating field of oceanic research. Using satellites, scientists have determined where to penetrate the seafloor with drill holes tens-of-thousands of feet deep.

After decades of research and exploration, there has been a dawning realization of the importance of the oceans. Many people no longer associate the high seas as a huge sewer where refuse, waste and garbage may be conveniently disposed. Renewed efforts in marine ecology educate the public on the dangers of pollution and overfishing. Scientists and politicians alike are asking what should be done to ensure the wise and safe use of the oceans' resources.

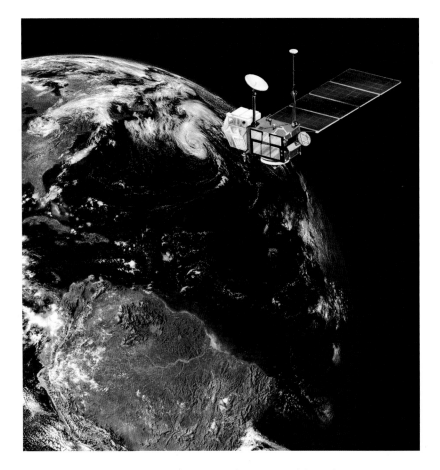

Satellites like the Topes/Poseidon (above) are used to help scientists explore the oceans of the world.

The Glomar Challenger *was used for drilling core samples.*

Chapter Two

PHYSICAL CHARACTERISTICS OF THE OCEAN

"WHO ENCLOSED THE SEA WITH DOORS, WHEN . . . I PLACED BOUNDARIES ON IT, AND I SET A BOLT AND DOORS, AND I SAID, 'THUS FAR SHALL YOU COME, BUT NO FARTHER; AND HERE SHALL YOUR PROUD WAVES STOP'?" JOB 38:8-11 (NASB).

THE COAST AND ITS SHORELINE

The temporary junction between sea and land is the shoreline. On nautical charts, the shoreline is the limit of high tides. The extent of the world's shoreline is approximately 275,000 miles (444,000 km). The region immediately behind the shoreline is the coast. Due to thousands of inlets, the Atlantic Ocean has more miles of shoreline than the Indian and Pacific Oceans put together.

The shorelines of the world receive their "romantic appearance" by the shaping influences of wave action, currents, and tides. Much of North America's western coast is called a

ONE OF THE FIRST EXPLORERS OF THE NORTH AMERICAN WILDERNESS, UPON VIEWING THE PACIFIC COAST FOR THE FIRST TIME, EXCLAIMED, "THE INUMERABLE ROCKS . . . AGAINST WHICH THE SEAS BREAK WITH GREAT FORCE GIVES THIS COAST A MOST ROMANTIC APPEARANCE." – WILLIAM CLARK, OF THE FAMOUS LEWIS AND CLARK EXPEDITION JANUARY 8, 1806 wave erosion coast, having characteristic steep cliffs, eroded by ocean waves. Water erosion also carves sea caves and arches along rocky coasts. After the heavy surf continuously pounds weak areas of the rock, tides and currents carry away the loosened portions. Other coasts include sand dune coasts and landslide coasts. Shorelines may also be altered by the action of oysters, mussels, other sea creatures, and various types of vegetation. Billions of coral polyps build coral islands in the Pacific (Gilbert and Marshall Islands, for example) and also coral reef coasts such as the Florida Keys.

Sea caves are carved by water erosion along rocky coasts.

Lining many miles of the world's shoreline are beaches composed of a sloping coast covered by sand (tiny sediment particles) or other loose material, such as pebbles. The beaches extend from the low-water line to the strip of land where plants can grow. Although most people think of beach sand as beige, sand actually comes in a variety of shades, from black volcanic sand found on some of the Hawaiian Islands to the nearly white sand of Pensacola Beach, Florida. The beach colors are due to the mineral composition of the sand grains or pebbles. Beaches are dynamic, for they constantly change with the weather. They may become narrow or grow wider depending on ocean conditions and storm, especially hurricane, severity. For this reason, there is always an element of risk when one purchases beachfront property!

The smooth line of beaches is broken by natural indentations forming areas like harbors, lagoons, estuaries and other important wetland areas. A harbor may be a naturally or artificially sheltered area of water with few or low waves. Harbors give protection for ships to anchor (moor) away from the more powerful breakers on the open shore. Artificial harbors are made of stone or steel breakwaters while natural harbors have "arms" of land that protect the inlet or bay. Many of the world's largest cities may be found next to a natural harbor or bay, where ships can load or unload their cargoes.

A lagoon or bay is a shallow body of brackish or ocean water generally separated from the ocean by a sandy ridge, coral reef, or barrier island. Lagoons are found along the Gulf of Mexico and the eastern coast of the United States. Sediments, such as sand carried by streams or rivers, gradually fill in the lagoon.

In contrast to many lagoons, fjords may be hundreds of feet deep. These arms of the sea may have formed after the Ice Age when rising seas flooded glacial valleys that ended in the ocean. Like many glacier-carved valleys, the sides of a fjord are U-shaped and steep. Fjords are also narrow whereas lagoons and bays can be quite wide.

Aerial view of salt water marsh

Estuaries form at the mouths of rivers where ocean water mixes with fresh water from the river. Due to this mixing, the water is brackish. Estuaries provide valuable feeding areas, breeding grounds, and habitat for birds, mammals, fish, and other wildlife, in effect acting as wildlife sanctuaries for a wide range of animals, some of them endangered species. These unique areas also act as nurseries for marine organisms, producers of valuable organic matter, filters for water, and flood control areas. Due to dwindling numbers of wildlife species that require this specific habitat, laws have been enacted to protect and preserve these valuable wetlands.

Both tidal and salt marshes are found along shorelines and in lagoons, bays and estuaries. The salt marsh at Cape Cod Bay is an example of one that is found where a river runs into the sea. Due to daily tidal activity at the mouth of the river, low waves from the sea constantly mix saltwater with the fresh water flowing downstream. Some coastal marshes, however, are primarily fresh-water tidal marshes. Whether fresh or brackish, the water flooding a tidal marsh is always affected by the tides. Because of the difference in salinity, different types of plants than those found in coastal fresh-water marshes grow in salt marshes. A salt marsh must be in an area protected from ocean waves. Only plants such as salt-meadow grass and cordgrass that are resistant to the effects of seawater inhabit salt marshes.

Typical salt marsh animals include sparrows, wrens, raccoons, mud crabs, fiddler crabs, ribbed mussels, and algae-eating snails. Although they may not be as interesting to look at as the ocean, salt marshes (and estuaries in general) are some of the most productive biological systems on Earth. This is due to large numbers of marine and land-based creatures that benefit from the living and decaying plant life.

CONTINENTAL MARGIN

The wide area between the continents' coasts and the deep sea floor is the continental margin. It consists of the continental shelf, continental slope, continental rise, and abyssal plain.

The continental shelf, composed of continental crust overlain by sediments, is the submerged land adjacent to a continent. It usually extends from the coast to a point at which the slope increases rapidly, typically a few tens of miles out to sea. However, the width of the continental shelf can vary, from one mile (1.6 km) in some areas of the Pacific to 750 miles (1,200 km) in the Arctic region.

The continental slope, which is defined as the true edge or side of the continent, begins at the edge of the continental shelf and reaches into the ocean's greater depth. The continental slope is steeper than the continental shelf, dropping from around 660 feet to 2¼ miles (200 m to 3.6 km) depth. The continental rise forms the transition from the abyssal plain to the outer edge of the continental slope.

Beyond the continental margin lie the fascinating features of the ocean deep — the basins, seamounts, ridges, and trenches. Oceanographers know of at least fifty areas of the ocean greater than 19,685 feet (6,000 m), or about 3½

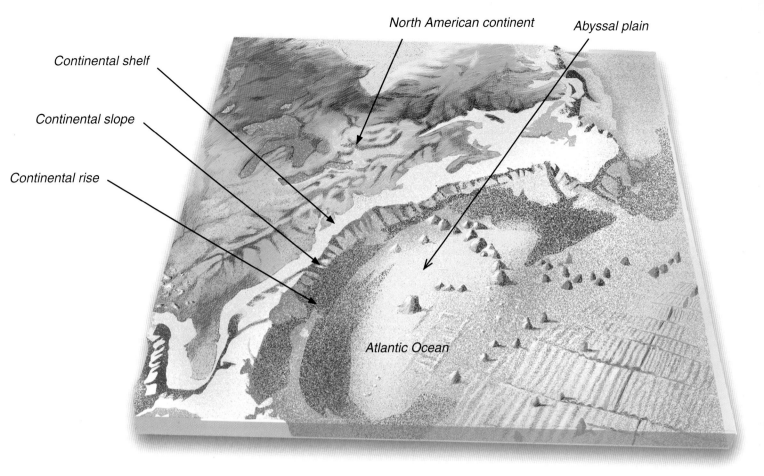

Continental shelf

Continental slope

Continental rise

North American continent

Abyssal plain

Atlantic Ocean

miles straight down! These are known as deep ocean basins. Although unseen because they are underwater, such basins, or abyssal plains, make up more than half of the earth's surface. They begin at the base of the continental slopes and extend, flatter than anyone has ever seen on land, mile after mile. Most of these plains have only a thin veneer of sediment, and occasionally sedimentary rock, resting primarily on one rock type — basalt. Abyssal benthic animals, which live permanently in or on the sea bottom, are found on these plains. These creatures include a type of brittle star that may be found on almost all deep sediments and the bizarre tripodfish with its long, curved, sensitive fins that aid in its capture of food.

Plains, islands, canyons, hills, volcanic cones, plateaus and active sections of seafloor spreading interrupt the flat expanses of these deep basins. All of these features of the undersea plain occupy the deepest sections of the ocean basins. Volcanic cones — structures with almost perfect conical shapes — have been found in virtually every area of the ocean floor. In 1993, oceanographers found a large concentration of active volcanoes along the South Pacific sea floor — some threatening eruption. This area, hundreds of square miles in extent, has over

1,000 seamounts and volcanic cones. Due to the lack of wind or pounding surf experienced by geologic features on land, some geologic features in the deep ocean remain as jagged and sharp as if they were formed yesterday. This is true of undersea ridges, cones and peaks. There is no wind or frost to smooth the geologic contours over the centuries; they are preserved, unchanged. However, some seamounts with peaks close to the surface had their tops eroded by wave action. These flat-topped seamounts are called "guyots."

TRENCHES

Located at the base of some continental slopes, trenches have relatively steep sides falling dramatically to the ocean

The average temperature at the bottom of most oceans is 35–37°F (2–3°C).

The average depth of the ocean is 12,451 feet (3,795 m), which is about 2½ miles down. This is five times the average height of land features above sea level!

13

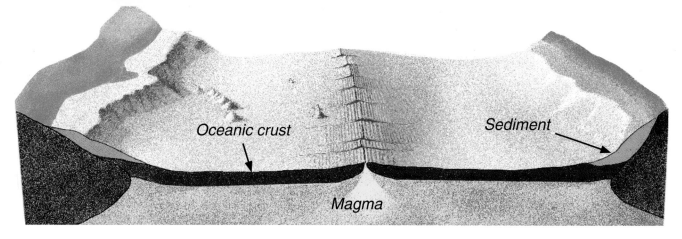

Magma surging up through cracks theoretically created by sea floor spreading

floor. These oceanic trenches, the deepest areas of the oceans, may be leftover subduction zones from crustal movement at the time of the Genesis flood. In geology, subduction is the theoretical process whereby one oceanic plate slides under another crustal plate. Subduction is believed to work by density. As the heavier plate descends steeply into the earth, the lighter, or less dense, of the two plates rides over the edge of the heavier plate. The long, narrow belt produced by this process is called the "subduction zone." It is in these areas that oceanic trenches (linear folds) form that can be approximately 1,500 miles (2,400 km) long, several miles deep, and as much as 70 miles (112 km) wide.

Oceanographers cite at least five trenches that are over 6 miles (10 km) deep. Trenches are geologically active with earthquakes and resulting tsunamis. Most volcanism associated with trenches occurs on the continent and not on the seafloor. However, many of the ocean's volcanic islands and seamounts are found in what are called "island arcs," bending chains of islands rising from the sea floor, usually paralleling the concave edges of an oceanic trench. The western Pacific has island arcs, as do the Aleutian Islands.

Near the island of Guam is the famous Mariana Trench located where the Pacific Plate descends under the leading edge of the Eurasian Plate. Measured at 36,201 feet — over 6.8 miles (11 km) deep, this trench is the deepest known spot in any ocean. In 1960, two brave men in the bathyscaph *Trieste* reached the Mariana Trench — a truly daring accomplishment! Other extensive trench regions around the world include the South Sandwich Trench between South America and Antarctica, the Peru-Chile Trench, and the Aleutian Trench.

OCEANIC RIDGES

Oceanic ridges are mountain ranges under the ocean, primarily composed of long crests of young basaltic rock. These mountain ranges are one of Earth's most remarkable features. If the world's water were taken away, these oceanic ridges would stand out more prominently than the most awesome mountains of Europe or Asia. The ridges extend 52,000 miles (84,000 km) as an underwater mountain chain that stretches almost completely around the world.

Occupying a third of the sea floor, the Mid-Atlantic Ridge snakes down the entire length of the Atlantic like the stitched seam of a baseball. In fact, the Mid-Atlantic Ridge goes straight through Iceland. Geologists call Iceland the most geologically active place on Earth with more vapor vents and hot springs than anywhere else. Volcanic activity

The Mariana Trench stretches 20% deeper than the world's highest mountain, Mount Everest, stands tall!

Japan

Japan Trench

along oceanic ridges could be plainly seen in 1963 with the violent formation of Iceland's new island, Surtsey. Its landforms, including "mature" looking beaches, are a challenge to a doctrine of geology (uniformitarianism) that states Earth's features form in a very slow, gradual manner.

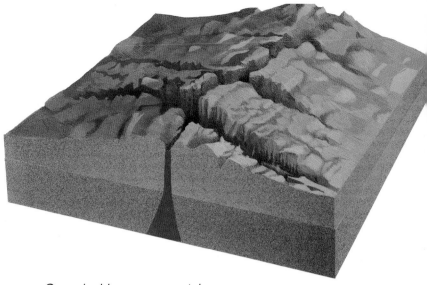

Oceanic ridges are mountain ranges under the ocean.

HYDROTHERMAL VENTS

The theoretical process of seafloor spreading may have accompanied subduction and continental movement during the Genesis flood. These spreading centers would result from the continents moving and pulling apart. As these areas of the ocean floor spread, super hot mantle material could surge up through the cracks in the mid-oceanic ridges.

In 1977, researchers aboard the submarine *Alvin* explored the ocean floor near the Galapagos Islands off the coast of Ecuador in South America. At 8,202 feet (2,500 m) down, they were amazed to see jets of black, toxic, mineral-rich water coming from the ocean floor. The 660°F (350°C) water spews from rocky 66-foot (20 m) tall chimneys. These unusual openings, or "black smoker chimneys," are called "hydrothermal vents." Scientists believe that as seawater seeps down through cracks in the ocean floor, it comes into contact with rocks heated by underground pockets of magma (molten rock).

Such hydrothermal vents, perhaps the most exciting features of the ocean floor, are found on some oceanic ridges in areas that are thought to be the remnant of seafloor spreading. These fascinating vents have been found off the coasts of Japan, Louisiana, California, Oregon, and

Washington. They are also found on the Juan de Fuca ridge and in the North Sea.

Scientists have also discovered a unique marine community of creatures associated with these vents. These creatures are characterized by high numbers of individuals and large body size. These strange animals include huge tubeworms 10 to 13 feet (3-4 m) long and giant white clams. Chemosynthetic bacteria, thriving on the hydrogen sulfide, are quite at home at these depths. Other creatures include translucent jellyfish attached to the rocks by a stalk and crabs and shrimp foraging, unhampered by their blindness. Exploration of these mysterious vent communities continues, with many questions yet to be answered.

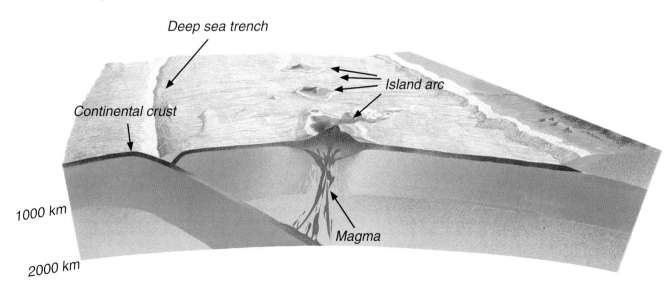

Island arcs generally run parallel to the concave edges of a deep trench.

Chapter Three
COMPOSITION OF THE OCEANS' WATERS

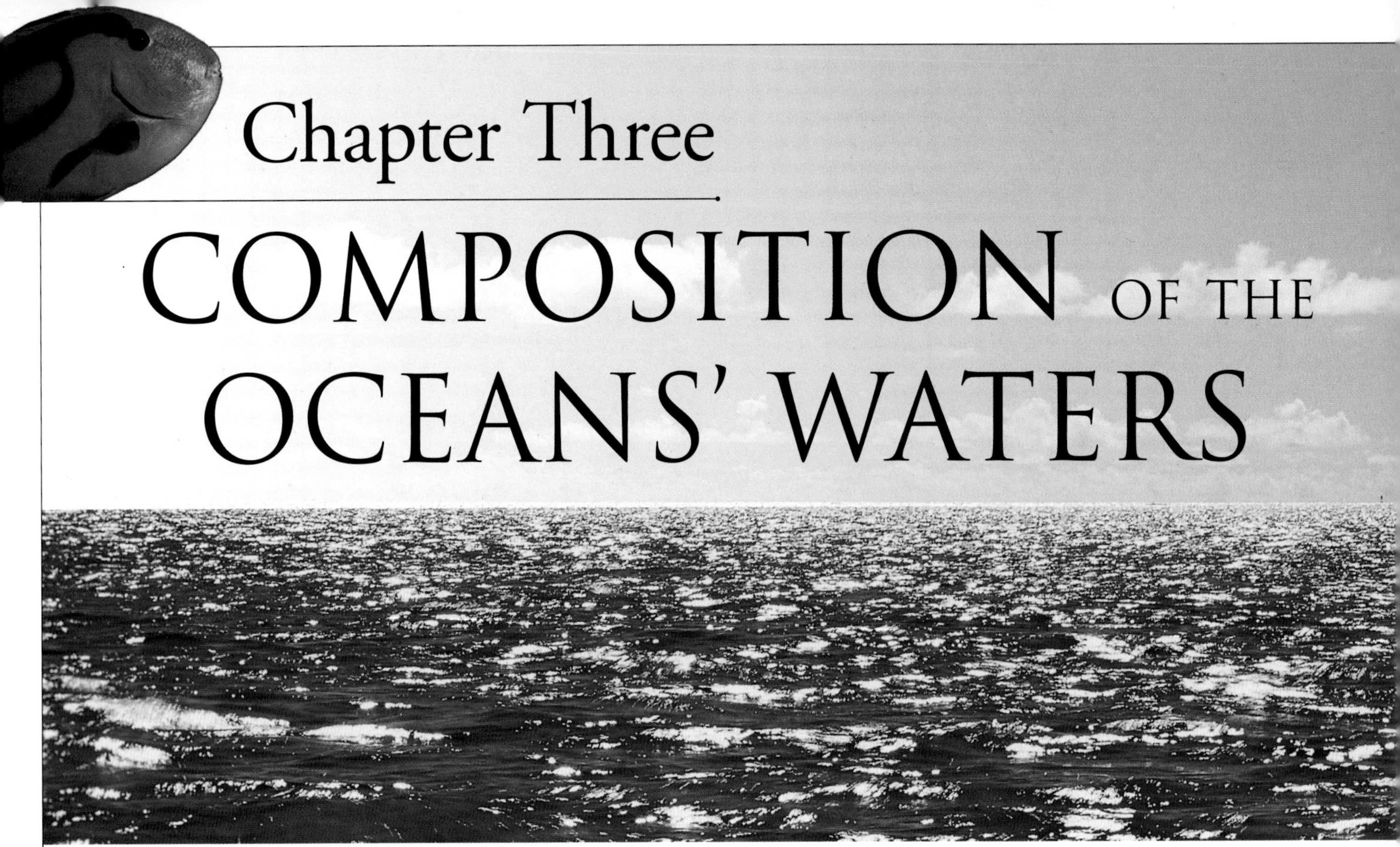

Creation scientists feel that the world before the Genesis flood was very different from the world after that catastrophe. For example, it is impossible to determine how full the oceans were at that time compared to the present. This is especially true considering the extent of crustal movements during and following the flood. Scripture suggests that originally, there may have been just one continent with mountains of low elevation and shallow ocean basins. The devastation during the worldwide flood (Genesis 6–9) changed all of that, producing the world we see today with its deep oceans and tall mountains. It is also impossible to find out how salty the pre-flood ocean waters were. It is very possible that the waters gathered into one place and called "seas" contained salts from the moment of their creation.

Elements of the Oceans *(per cubic mile of water)*

Oxygen - 4,037,000,000 tons

Hydrogen - 509,000,000 tons

Chlorine - 89,500,000 tons

Sodium - 49,500,000 tons

Magnesium - 6,125,000 tons

Sulfur - 4,420,000 tons

Calcium - 1,880,000 tons

Potassium - 1,790,000 tons

Bromine - 306,000 tons

Carbon - 132,000 tons

Other - less than 100,000 tons (including gold, which is only 38 pounds per cubic mile of water)

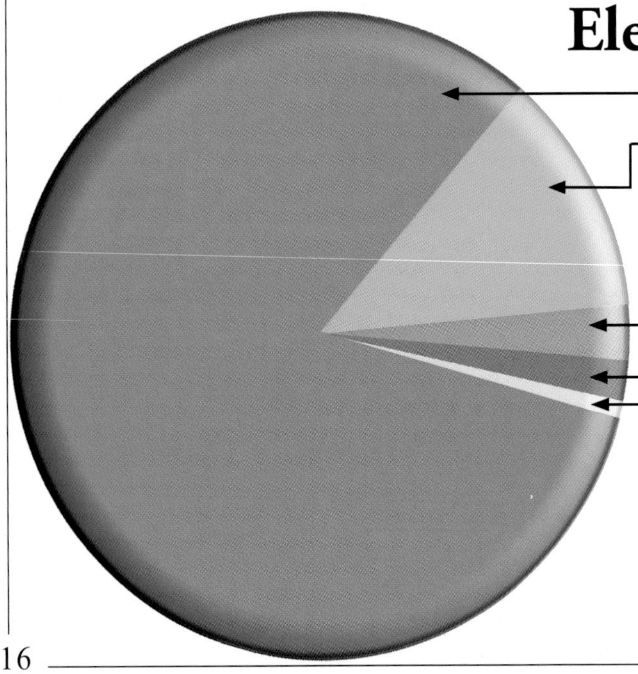

THE SEA'S SALT

Approximately 97% of all water on the surface of the earth is seawater. Seawater differs from fresh water mainly because it is salty. Salinity is a measurement of the total amount of the dissolved solids or minerals in water. Every 1,000 grams of ocean water contains 35 grams of salt and 965 grams of water.

A cubic mile of ocean water contains 166 million tons of salt. If all the sea water evaporated, the 46 quadrillion tons of salt (sodium chloride) contained in the oceans of the world would cover the surface area of the seven continents with almost 420 feet (130 m) of salt.

Many nations have always looked to the oceans to provide food for their meals, yet the very waters from which these provisions come from are not fit to drink. This seems strange since seawater is made of water and salt, both of which animals and people need to survive! Though scientists cannot establish how salty the waters were to begin with, they do know that the oceans are becoming saltier with time. Where does the salt being added to the seawater come from? Runoff from surface weathering, as well as chemicals in the earth, gives the oceans their salty character. The most significant source of dissolved salts is erosion and weathering of crustal rocks. Another minor source are chemicals called "excess volatiles." Found in the deep layers of the earth, these chemicals include fluorine, hydrogen, carbon dioxide and sulfur.

A dip in seawater will get you as wet as a bath in fresh water. However, if you were to drink seawater over days or possibly weeks, you would die of dehydration (severe loss of water). Why? The answer involves the miraculous pair of bean-shaped organs called the kidneys. These amazing structures were designed by the Creator to do a wide number of critical functions, such as regulate the amount of water and salt in the blood, keeping them at very specific levels. More than *one million* tiny filtering units in each kidney remove excess salt from the body. To remove this surplus salt requires a plentiful supply of fresh water. (That is why you get thirsty when you eat too many salty potato chips.) If you drank a liter of saltwater, your kidneys would require at least *three* liters of fresh, pure water to wash out the excess salt. Therefore, people adrift on the ocean dare not drink seawater; it speeds up the rate of dehydration and leads to a slow and painful death.

Naval aviators face a problem of how to get fresh water when they ditch their plane at sea. Each person's survival kit includes an ingenious desalination kit composed of a small cake of resin and activated charcoal that soaks up salt by a process called "ion exchange." The aviators simply put seawater into a plastic bag and then add the cake of charcoal and resin to absorb the salt. The resulting freshwater still tastes terrible, but it is mostly salt-free and will keep them alive until rescued.

How can animals in the open ocean survive without drinking fresh water? God in His wisdom has equipped many creatures, such as seabirds and reptiles, with specially designed salt glands that remove excess salt. Marine fish, too, have been designed to eliminate large amounts of excess salt through their gills and kidneys while conserving their internal body water.

In the *Challenger* expedition of the 1800s, naturalists took 1,718 samples of seawater from a number of oceans and various depths to make a comparison of the salt content. What do you suppose they found? Amazingly, the chemical

Every 1,000 grams of ocean water contains 35 grams of salt.

REFINING SALT FOR CONSUMPTION

Centuries ago, salt was — ounce for ounce — as precious as gold. It was so valuable that salt was even used as currency. Countries around the Mediterranean Sea used salt cakes as currency, and in early China, they used salt coins! Many of the first caravan routes and roads of Egypt and Spain were made for the purpose of carrying salt. Even cities such as Venice and Pisa in Italy developed due to trade in salt. Throughout human history, this precious commodity was used to flavor food as well as preserve it. Dried, salted meats resist decay — a necessity in unrefrigerated societies even today.

Many years ago, salt was so valuable that many roads were established for salt caravans to transport this valuable commodity.

makeup of ocean water is the same everywhere. Keep in mind that the entire ocean is not salty. For example, the volume of water South America's Amazon River discharges into the Atlantic is about ten times the flow volume of the Mississippi River. The Amazon waters at this point are also nearly as pure as distilled water! As the large volume of fresh water mixes with the salty ocean water, the salinity decreases in the ocean surrounding the mouth of the Amazon. The Amazon pours so much water into the Atlantic that the water is still fresh a hundred miles away from the shore.

The oceans have always been an important source of salt. People have been extracting salt from seawater for many centuries by evaporation, the oldest method of extraction. Today, salt is extracted through a series of large evaporation ponds. Salt formed from this process is often called solar salt. The southern end of San Francisco Bay has evaporation ponds, and more may be found near the Great Salt Lake in Utah and in the Bahamas. This method is also popular in India, China, France, and Japan.

SALT FROM OCEAN WATER EVAPORATION

Seawater is a dilute solution of a number of salts including calcium, potassium, sodium, and magnesium. Seawater also includes ions such as chloride, sulfate, bicarbonate and bromide. As pure water (ion-free) is evaporated from seawater by the sun, salt and minerals are left behind, forming a white, solid, crystal-like precipitate, or brine, on the shoreline. (This should not be confused with white sand, which cannot dissolve in water.) Out in the ocean, solar energy causes great quantities of pure water to evaporate from the

Utah salt flats

18

surface. This water vapor accumulates to form clouds while the minerals and salt remain in the ocean.

FRESH WATER FROM THE OCEAN

Scientists tell us that less than one-tenth of one percent (0.017%) of the water found on Earth is fresh, liquid, and available for use by people. In some parts of the world, pure fresh water often costs more per liter than gasoline!

American military ships, such as nuclear aircraft carriers, use desalination plants to produce fresh water. This water is used by the ship's thousands of sailors and for the steam catapults, which are used to launch aircraft.

Much research has gone into finding inexpensive, more efficient ways to remove salt from sea and brackish water — a process called "desalination." Worldwide, from West Africa to California, over 12,500 desalination plants produce 7.9 billion gallons (29 billion liters) of fresh water each day. The country of Saudi Arabia has the world's largest desalination plant, that produces 166 million gallons (630 million liters) per day.

Perhaps the most imaginative suggestion to meet freshwater demands in major cities was proposed in the late 1960s.

Scientists once suggested that tugboats take advantage of the mighty Humboldt Current to tow a 10-mile (16 km) long iceberg from the Antarctic to be grounded on an offshore shoal off thirsty Los Angeles. Though it would lose half its bulk during the yearlong transit, the berg would still provide about 300 billion gallons (1.2 trillion l) of fresh water — enough to last the city about a month! Can you think of several reasons why this was never attempted — and probably never will be? What gave the scientists the idea in the first place for recommending an Antarctic iceberg?

Icebergs towed from polar regions could be possible sources of fresh water.

Icebergs

Imagine watching an *ice sheet larger than the state of Delaware* break free and crash into the Amundsen Sea off Antarctica! That is just what happened in March 2002. Scientists later reported that this 500-billion-ton ice sheet shattered and set thousands of icebergs adrift. Icebergs are massive floating chunks of frozen fresh water that have originated from fallen snow and have broken off an ice sheet or glacier.

Glaciers are great masses of snow turned to ice that flow like a large frozen river and move slowly and steadily downhill. The rate of a glacier's movement changes during different times of the year, at different stages of the glacier's existence, and even varies at different places in the glacier itself. Though the average flow rate is less than 3 feet (1 m) per day, surges may move glaciers downhill at more than 10 feet (3 m) per day. At least one glacier's surge speed was clocked at 315 feet (105 m) per day!

Such glacial ice covers roughly six million square miles of Earth's land. When glacier fronts reach the water, huge chunks of ice break off to form icebergs which then float away to sea. Though the speed of a drifting berg depends mainly upon the wind and currents, the iceberg's own size and shape, the obstacles in its path, and its location in the ocean also influence its movement. Although icebergs, like glaciers, have occasional bursts of speed, their wandering life can also include motionless periods. When on the move, they often travel at rates between 4 to 10 miles (6 to 16 km) per day. Whenever the bergs move into warmer waters, the greater warmth causes them to rapidly melt. The warm waters of the Gulf Stream can melt a 150,000-ton iceberg in ten days or less.

Icebergs originate in the two polar regions of the world and the two kinds differ in their formation and appearance. Small icebergs ("growlers") may calve, or break off, from larger ones.

The classic pinnacle iceberg, usually seen in movies or documentaries, is formed in the Arctic and has projections much like a castle-turret and other craggy features. The glaciers from which many of these icebergs come are found in western Greenland. Northern icebergs usually float for some months across Baffin Bay and Davis Straight to the Grand Banks off Newfoundland where they take about two years to melt.

Icebergs formed from the Antarctic ice sheet are more regular in shape than those formed in the Arctic. The Antarctic shelf, which is about 5 million square miles (13 million square km), slowly overflows its land support to

Iceberg at Gerlache Strait, Antarctica

The Titanic *struck a pinnacle iceberg, similar to this one, and sank on its maiden voyage.*

form a layer of ice on the sea. With no land to support the weight of the ice, huge ice pieces break off to form broad, flat icebergs that may be 20 miles long (32 km) and weigh over 990,000 tons. The commonly flat, long, and table-like shape gives these bergs the name of tabular icebergs.

Aside from their awesome size, Southern Hemisphere icebergs are less dangerous than those in the Northern Hemisphere. Water becomes less dense when it freezes, which explains why ice floats. Whether you observe an ice cube or an iceberg, you will notice that most of its bulk is under the water's surface. Since about 90 percent of the mass of an iceberg lies below the water line, it poses an unseen threat to ships that venture too close. Icebergs are a serious threat to shipping, especially during the months of April, May and June. One of the most disastrous events in maritime history was on the night of April 14-15, 1912. The White Star line RMS *Titanic,* then the largest ship afloat, struck an underwater edge of a pinnacle iceberg on its maiden voyage. Hours later, the mighty *Titanic* sank, resulting in the loss of over 1,500 lives in the Arctic waters.

The U.S. Coast Guard and the International Ice Patrol (IIP) now use ice patrol boats and keep a constant watch in iceberg areas. How do scientists of the IIP go about actually predicting the movement of these dangerous mountains of floating ice? They keep a close eye on the weather and use the sound application of math, scientific theory, and ocean current charts to predict the movement of icebergs.

21

Chapter Four

TIDES, WAVES, AND CURRENTS

As long as man has gone to sea in ships, he has been fascinated and frightened by the powerful and restless bodies of water. People enjoy sitting for hours gazing at bluish-green breakers as they crash and foam on rock outcrops off northern California. Swimmers off the East Coast do not realize that some of the water washing over them took years to cover vast distances, even from Antarctica. Ship captains are careful to follow tidal charts as their vessels leave a seaport and then "hitch a ride" on one of many powerful ocean currents that are going their way. These mighty ocean movements may be placed in three major categories: tides, waves, and currents.

TIDES

From ancient times, seafaring people have noticed that the level of the sea at the shoreline changed throughout the day and that these changes were related to near-shore tidal currents. Keeping track of these changes was vitally important in controlling the movement of ships into and out of harbors and river inlets to the sea. The fear of grounding a ship against uncharted reefs or sandbars would always push captains to enter or leave port near high tide. Not only that, but the flow of water is a powerful force, and sailors wanted to use this energy to their favor. This was particularly true when the primary forces used by ships were wind and oar. However, the huge powerful vessels of today still respect the tides. The mighty power of tidal currents can easily cause disasters if not heeded. Indeed, some places have such huge tidal ranges that modern technology is of no help. One of the most famous of these is the Bay of Fundy, located between Nova Scotia and New Brunswick. There, the highest tides in the world rise and fall almost 53 feet (16 meters) twice a day, every day! That is around 254 billion tons of saltwater making its way in and out of the bay with enough force to spin a battleship.

Around the 13th century, predictions of tidal motion had been made based on repeated observations of the rise and fall of the ocean each day, and these changes had rightly been related to the motion (phases) of the moon. However, it was not until Sir Isaac Newton (undoubtedly the world's greatest scientist, and a creationist) applied his law of gravitation to the tides that prediction methods could be systematically developed. These methods have led to publishing tide tables which are critical for coastal nations to use in sea borne commerce, military coastal actions, salvage, dredging, and a host of related activities.

The major tide-causing forces are the gravitational effects that the moon and the sun have on the planet. Bodies, of course, cannot feel their gravitational pulls, because their pulls are very small with respect to the gravitational pull felt from the earth. However, the forces are real enough and big enough over the distance of an entire ocean basin to cause shifting of the water and the tides that result. To be sure, tidal forces do occur in the air (very slight) and in the land (slighter still), but it is in the ocean that one sees the greatest result and the greatest impact on life.

It is not known what gravity "is" — that is, what causes one mass to be attracted to another mass. However, the force can be measured and described as a function of the mass of the objects involved and the distance between them. Interestingly, the farther apart things are, the lower the force of gravity is between them. Because the moon is much closer to the earth than the sun is, the moon exerts a much greater force on the earth than does the sun. The moon's force is about twice as much as the sun's, in spite of the sun's incredibly huge mass. Stars and other planets also exert gravitational forces on the earth, but these are so small that they are negligible. Predictions of the tides, therefore, need to primarily incorporate the motion of the sun and the moon with respect to the earth.

To understand how this works, first consider just the impact of the moon's gravitational pull on the earth. Imagine being in outer space above the North Pole of the earth. Pretend that there are no landmasses. You would see the earth rotating counterclockwise, one rotation per day. The water would be of uniform depth as the earth's gravity (acting from the earth's center of mass) is equal everywhere, pulling the water in toward the center of mass. In addition, the earth's centripetal acceleration is also equal everywhere, and in balance.

Now, add the moon to this model. The moon's gravitational pull causes the water to bulge out on the side of the earth closest to the moon. This bulge creates higher water levels on the side affected. Consider the mass balance of the whole earth-moon system. The center of the earth's mass is at its core. Adding the moon actually causes the system's center of mass to be no longer at the core of the earth. The center of mass has moved toward the side of the earth closest to the moon (about one fourth of the earth's diameter). This means that the water on the side

Varied marine life can be found in tidal pools at low tide.

of the earth away from the moon receives a smaller gravitational pull from the earth (because the center of mass has moved away from that side of the earth). But, because the centripetal acceleration has not changed, a bulge of water forms on the side away from the moon as well. Since the total amount of water stays the same, higher water levels on two sides are balanced by lower water levels between them. All things being equal, this would mean that at any point on the earth, you would experience two high tides (one for the side toward the moon and one for the side opposite the moon) and two low tides (the two sides with the lower water levels between the bulges) each day.

Low tide

Now, throw the sun into the model. During the new moon, the gravitational pull of the sun will be on the same side as the moon. During full moon, the sun is pulling from the side opposite the moon. At both of these times, the pull of the sun adds to the pull of the moon and creates higher high tides (and of course, lower low tides). These are called "spring tides." When the sun and the moon line up this way, it is called "syzygy." Alternatively, when the sun, earth and moon form a 90-degree angle, it is called "quadrature." At that point, the sun counteracts the impact of the moon, so there are lower high tides and higher low tides. These are called "neap tides."

This means that in a perfect model, two high tides and two low tides occur each day, but over a year the height of the tides will oscillate from the highest high and lowest low tides (spring tides at syzygy) to the lowest high and highest low tides (neap tides at quadrature).

Now when reality is added in, it really makes things complicated. Consider that:
• different oceans have different sizes and depths;
• land mass shapes are different;
• the moon does not revolve exactly in the same plane as the earth revolves round the sun;
• the orbits of the moon about the earth and the earth about the sun are not perfect circles but ellipses;
• the cycle of the moon's revolution about the earth is about 18.6 years;

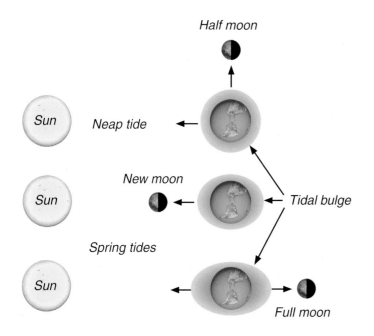

• with the motion of the moon in the same direction as the rotation of the earth, the actual period of the high to low tide is not 12 hours, but 12.4 hours.

About 65 of these modifiers exist, and they impact the expected two high and two low tides per day (called "semi-diurnal" tides). Now, some places like Liverpool, England, follow this pattern; but the semi-diurnal pattern on west coast locations in the United States differs. In these places two highs and two lows still occur per day; but one of the highs is much higher than the other high tide, and one of the lows is much lower than the other low tide. Still other places along the east coast of Asia have only one high and one low tide per day.

On the island of Tahiti, the difference between high and low tide varies by only one foot or less, regardless of the moon's relationship to Earth.

Fortunately, comprehensive tide tables have been created for the entire world and automatic tide measuring devices have been installed at a host of locations around the world to help validate and refine our tide models of the world.

WAVES

What is the difference between tides and waves? While tides are very long waves that move across the entire ocean, winds disturbing just the top layer of water form most waves. (Some waves are formed by underwater geologic activity.) The surf along the shoreline is produced by a combination of factors: wind strength, tides, and the length and depth of the particular continental shelf. Although waves can be seen all across the ocean, the near-shore surf is more obvious as it pounds against land.

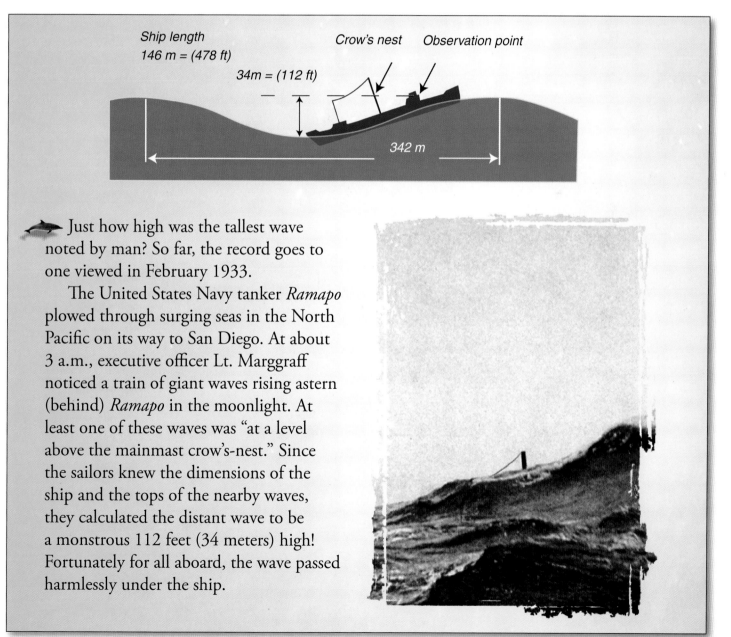

Ship length
146 m = (478 ft)

Crow's nest   Observation point

34m = (112 ft)

342 m

Just how high was the tallest wave noted by man? So far, the record goes to one viewed in February 1933.

The United States Navy tanker *Ramapo* plowed through surging seas in the North Pacific on its way to San Diego. At about 3 a.m., executive officer Lt. Marggraff noticed a train of giant waves rising astern (behind) *Ramapo* in the moonlight. At least one of these waves was "at a level above the mainmast crow's-nest." Since the sailors knew the dimensions of the ship and the tops of the nearby waves, they calculated the distant wave to be a monstrous 112 feet (34 meters) high! Fortunately for all aboard, the wave passed harmlessly under the ship.

The rhythmic rise and fall of the ocean's surface generated by wave movement is felt most dramatically if you ride in a boat or wade out from shore. Waves are really motions that carry the *energy* of the sea but not the *water*. In other words, the water itself has no forward motion as the wave passes through it.

You can see how this occurs by doing a simple experiment. Tie one end of a long rope to a solid object waist-high and then pull the other end of the rope back about 10 feet (33 m) or more, leaving a bit of slack in the rope. Move the end of the rope up and down sharply. The energy produced passes from one section of the rope to the other as a wave, but the rope itself does not move away from you. Nevertheless, the vigorous rope movement shows that energy is present.

Likewise, a cork bobbing on waves demonstrates that, although the cork moves only slightly as waves pass under it, it stays more-or-less in place. In other words, the wave*form* travels, but the water itself does not. A good example would be summer in southern California with the surf breaking from the south. Incredibly, this energy — not the water — has traveled 6,000 miles (9,654 km) from winter storms near New Zealand where it was generated. As the advancing swell starts to drag on the California continental shelf, it causes the water to move with it; the crest topples, producing great waves and pounding breakers. Surf's up, Dude!

Surf waves vary in size depending upon the steepness of the coast, the height of the tide, and storm activity. The famous surf on the north shore of Oahu, Hawaii, produces 20-foot (66 m) waves in the winter. Wind waves, in comparison, are often less than 10 feet (3 m) high and are found in the open ocean, having been produced by the transfer of wind energy onto the water's surface. Instruments called wave meters measure the direction, length, and height of waves.

Tsunami is the Japanese word for "harbor wave." This term refers to what used to be called a "tidal wave." These large movements of the ocean are caused by various events, such as underwater landslides, hurricanes, volcanic eruptions, or underwater faulting from an earthquake. If the earthquake is severe enough, it could possibly result in a tsunami that can travel at speeds just under 550 miles (890 km) per hour in the open sea, depending on the depth of water. A tsunami can pass under a boat in the open ocean without notice! Scientists using seismographs can pick up seismic sea waves produced by an earthquake and can then determine where and when the faulting occurred. Although a tsunami becomes unnoticeable as it spreads out, it becomes destructive near shore where friction

Destruction from the tsunami that hit Kodiak Island, Alaska

fountains of the great deep broken up" (Genesis 7:11), meaning that additional water locked in the earth's crust became part of the great flood waters. This statement is important! Notice that, when describing the flood, the Bible first mentions "the fountains of the great deep." The forty days and forty nights of rain ("windows of heaven") are mentioned second. The massive seismic activity (earthquakes) caused by the fountains of the great deep breaking up would have generated some very large tsunamis. Large waves would then be striking and shaping land formations before the land was finally covered with floodwaters. You can be sure that the occupants of the ark, guided by God's unseen hand, rode safely away from the areas of such violence.

with the sea bottom slows it down and the water "piles up." This may happen thousands of miles away from the actual earthquake.

The power of this surging water is amazing. In April 1946, Scotch Cap lighthouse in the Alaskan Aleutian Islands was completely destroyed by tsunami waves over 100 feet (30 m) in height. The light in the five-story steel-reinforced concrete structure had previously sat 90 feet (27 m) above sea level.

The 1883 volcanic eruption of the island of Krakatoa, a small South Pacific island near Java, caused some of the most destructive tsunamis ever known. "More than 100 feet high and with a velocity in excess of 50 miles an hour, they ravaged the nearby coasts of Java and Sumatra. In places, they raged inland for 1,000 yards and were still 30-feet high. They swept away entire towns and villages, almost 300 of them."

In the past, tsunamis struck shoreline communities without the inhabitants ever knowing that destruction was looming. Today, scientists use monitoring systems to track tsunamis in the Pacific Ocean in order to give advanced warning to people living on shores distant from the tsunami's source.

The most cataclysmic account of the forces of water is described in the book of Genesis. Scripture teaches that on "the same day were all the

Ocean currents

In May of 1990, when the container ship *Hansa Carrier* was bound for Seattle with dozens of boxcar-sized containers on deck, a violet storm blew up in northern Pacific waters. In the middle of the storm, several

wave energy

A cork floating on top of the water shows that waves pass through the water, but the water itself does not move.

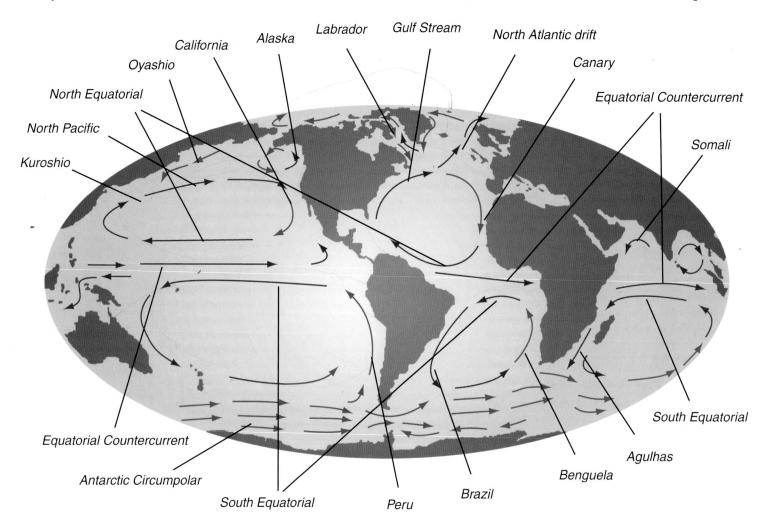

Map of the earth's major ocean currents. The blue arrows represent cold currents, and the red arrows show warm currents. The warm and cold temperatures are relative to the surrounding waters.

North Equatorial

Oyashio

California

Alaska

Labrador

Gulf Stream

North Atlantic drift

Canary

Equatorial Countercurrent

North Pacific

Kuroshio

Somali

Equatorial Countercurrent

Antarctic Circumpolar

South Equatorial

Peru

Brazil

Benguela

Agulhas

South Equatorial

containers washed overboard — releasing nearly 80,000 pairs of athletic shoes and workboots into the ocean! Half a year later, beachcombers from British Columbia to Oregon were treated to hundreds of expensive shoes. The saltwater had not ruined them so people began to exchange shoes because matching pairs had not been attached when they were lost overboard. At least one tubeworm-encrusted shoe ended up on display in a local science center. Scientists were quite interested in this event, because the shoes followed the currents of the North Pacific gyre, giving oceanographers a better idea of its features.

An even more amusing event happened on January 10, 1992, when a cargo container full of 29,000 plastic bathtub toys spilled from a freighter into the North Pacific. Released from their cage, the yellow ducks, green frogs, blue turtles, and red beavers began an unplanned though eventful journey that ended up assisting scientific research. Between 1992 and 1993, hundreds of the toys landed on the shores of Alaska.

Eleven years later, news reports indicated that the toys were being looked for in the North Atlantic! Why? The current carrying some of the toys to the Alaskan shores would have taken others far enough north that they could have become frozen in the Arctic icepack. The little hitchhikers would then travel with the ice until their section finally reached and melted into the North Atlantic.

As these two stories illustrate, the waters of the oceans are in constant movement. A basic premise of hydraulics tells us that water can virtually not be compressed. Therefore, water moving one direction displaces and sends water somewhere else. This is what is seen in the vast choreography of ocean currents.

Ocean currents are massive movements of water beneath or at the surface of the oceans. They differ from the water around them in salinity and temperature. Like rivers within the larger ocean, currents occur on a huge scale, with tremendous amounts of water carried over thousands of miles, sometimes in enormous circles *half an ocean in extent*. It was once thought that currents were simply large, traceable movements of ocean waters. Now, with more sophisticated equipment, oceanographers realize currents are very complex. The path seawater takes in its travels from the surface to the deep ocean and back looks like a huge conveyer belt twisting through the world's ocean basins. Scientists estimate that it may take 1,000 years for the "conveyer belt" to make one complete circuit. In their part of the belt, deep-water currents creep along, taking centuries to complete. It may take 600 years before deep water reaches the surface again. Conversely, some wind-swept surface waters take only months to cover the same distance.

Currents move mainly because of winds, the rotation of the earth (Coriolis effect), and the sun's heat. Convection, directly associated with the sun's energy, involves heat being transferred from the atmosphere to the ocean. Such a process keeps the earth's temperature relatively constant by cooling, heating, mixing, and transporting ocean waters. Counterclockwise currents are produced in the Southern Hemisphere and clockwise currents in the Northern Hemisphere.

Marine currents belong to two basic categories, surface and subsurface (undercurrents). Large, continuous circulatory systems of surface currents called gyres occur in the Pacific, Atlantic and Antarctic Oceans. In fact, the Antarctic gyre links all the major oceans together. Prevailing winds and the earth's rotation (Coriolis effect) keep gyres in constant motion. All three major oceans — the Pacific, Atlantic and Indian — show a similar pattern of circulation, with the Pacific having sluggish, deeper flow patterns. Subsurface currents flow in the opposite direction from the main current. These undercurrents can be found under most major currents.

Some currents are dangerous to humans. Popularly — though incorrectly — called "riptides," rip currents are strong, narrow

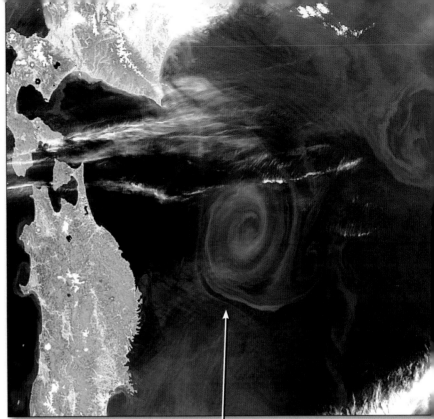

A large gyre off the coast of Japan

surface currents that carry large amounts of water back out to sea. These currents, which sometimes appear instantaneously, can form where two areas of strong surf meet or where obstructions like sandbars, piers, or the shoreline's shape affect the water flow. Swimmers should be very careful for these dangerous currents can carry people as fast as two miles (3 km) an hour. A swimmer caught in a rip current should not panic, but stay calm and *swim parallel to the beach* out of the narrow current's pull.

An undertow is a type of current that is not as dangerous to swimmers. Undertows occur after a breaker crashes on the beach. The water rushing back to the

The arrows showing flow away from the beach represent the dangerous rip currents.

ocean flows as a slender sheet along the bottom beneath incoming swells and breakers. A person can feel it drawing sand from under toes and feet as he stands in the surf.

Major currents

The best-known and most intensively studied current continues to be the Gulf Stream. The Gulf Stream is composed of all three types of currents: surface, subsurface and countercurrent. This massive current, or "river in the ocean," is a well-defined, swift movement of warm water that originates north of Grand Bahama Island where the Antilles Current and Florida Current meet. From there, it follows the eastern coast of North America to the Grand Banks along the Canadian coast. At this point, it combines with the Labrador Current and flows eastward as the North Atlantic Current, its deep blue color contrasting with the green of the surrounding waters. The warmer waters of the Gulf Stream explain why Great Britain experiences mild weather and heavy rainfall even though that country is situated close to the Arctic Circle. A branch of the Gulf Stream system is also the primary factor for the relatively mild climate of northern Norway.

Another major ocean current is the Kuroshio Current in the northwestern Pacific. Both its temperature and its salt content are higher than average seawater. This current, also called the "black stream," can be thought of as the counterpart to the Gulf Stream. It affects weather patterns that result in nourishing rains and clouds for Japan's southern coasts as well as the coasts of British Columbia, Washington and Oregon.

The Humboldt Current, or Peru Current, is a frigid, shallow movement originating near the South Pole and flowing slowly northward along the coasts of northern Chile

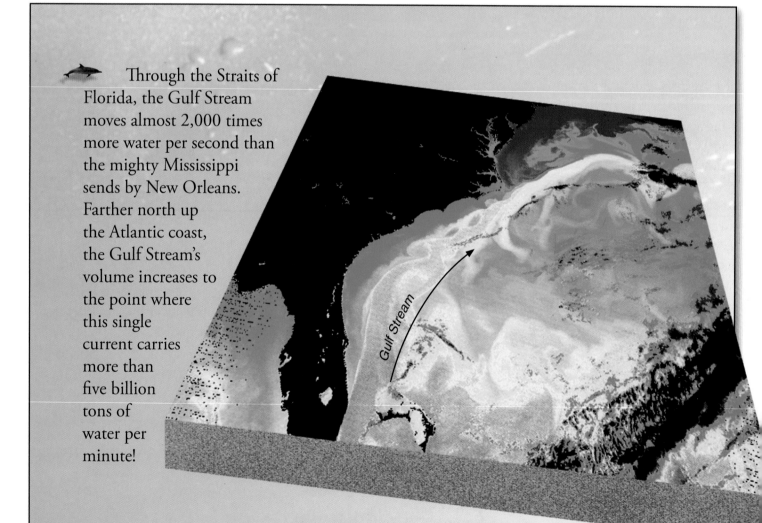

Through the Straits of Florida, the Gulf Stream moves almost 2,000 times more water per second than the mighty Mississippi sends by New Orleans. Farther north up the Atlantic coast, the Gulf Stream's volume increases to the point where this single current carries more than five billion tons of water per minute!

Gulf Stream

Wind

Continent

Cold water rises

The arrows in this diagram show the flow of the ocean water during upwelling.

WHIRLPOOLS & OCEAN CURRENTS

A whirlpool is a rapidly revolving ocean current or eddy that is caused by one or more of the following: the meeting of opposing tides or currents, the wind action on the water, or friction between the water and the configuration of the shore or seafloor. Whirlpools usually occur in shallow, partially enclosed waters swiftly moving between islands. The Old Sow, a whirlpool between Maine and New Brunswick, claims the title of "the largest whirlpool in the Western Hemisphere." However, two better-known whirlpools are the *Charybdis* (called *Garofalo* today) in the Strait of Messina between Italy

A nutrient upwelling off Costa Rica is shown in dark green.

and Peru, bringing fog and cool temperatures to these two countries. Various fish, dolphins, and whales accompany the Humboldt Current because it carries an abundant load of nutrients and causes an upwelling of water rich in fertilizing minerals such as phosphates. These minerals nourish a rich population of tiny marine life upon which larger animals then feed, an example of a food pyramid. Every few years, however, the Humboldt Current changes, shifting unexpectedly seaward. The important upwelling ceases and warm waters move in, killing the plankton at the base of the food pyramid. When this happens, many fish and birds starve or go elsewhere for food. As a result, the guano (fertilizer) and fishing industries also suffer severely.

Nutrient upwelling, the upward movement of water below the surface, is of great climatic and biological importance. Upwelling encourages flourishing marine life near the surface by bringing nutrient-rich waters up from 200 to 980 feet (60 to 300 m) below the surface. In coastal regions, upwelling is mostly wind driven. As coastal surface waters are pushed about by winds, deeper, colder water flows upward to take its place. This process occurs intermittently along the coast of North America and along the western coasts of Africa and South America. Upwelling also occurs in the equatorial Pacific Ocean where the Coriolis force causes the trade winds to push large ocean currents away from each other.

and Sicily and the *Maelstrom* in the sound between the Norwegian islands of Moskenesøy and Værøy. Although literature of the past greatly exaggerated the strength and danger of the whirlpools, sailors still navigate the strong currents with caution. Whirlpools are fascinating phenomena and can be read about in Homer's *The Odyssey* and Edgar Allan Poe's "A Descent into the Maelstrom."

MEASURING THE CURRENTS

One of the first people to conduct a scientific study of currents and emphasize their importance to seafarers was Benjamin Franklin. He recognized the problem of the long transit from England to the American colonies (east to west) and that it took two weeks less to travel from west to east. When he asked his cousin Timothy Folger, a New England whaling captain, about this discrepancy, Franklin learned that American sea captains sailed their ships to take advantage of a great current running eastward across the North Atlantic. That current is now known as the Gulf Stream. Franklin had his cousin draw a map of the Gulf Stream's surface currents and their effects on ships. He suggested to the British captains that they sail through this stream only as they return to England, but the British sailors ignored this strange chart for years. In later years, during voyages to and from England, Franklin himself took daily measurements of the current's temperature and described the water's color and plant life.

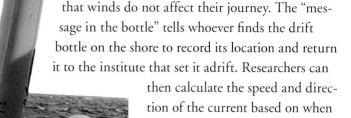

*Current meter ready
for deployment*

An old, but reliable and accurate, method of studying the direction and speed of an ocean current are drift bottles. Oceanographers release weighted bottles to float just below the water's surface so that winds do not affect their journey. The "message in the bottle" tells whoever finds the drift bottle on the shore to record its location and return it to the institute that set it adrift. Researchers can then calculate the speed and direction of the current based on when the bottle was released and when it was found.

Oceanographers also use current meters or flow meters to measure important ocean currents, both on the surface and below, from a fixed position. The most popular device is the Ekman flow meter which takes its measurements as it is suspended from a moored ship. The current turns a paddle impeller (wheel) in the meter, then a dial counter monitors the number of revolutions, while a directional vane determines the direction of flow.

Computers and electronic technology have advanced so that oceanographers may now sense the subtle electromagnetic force produced by the ocean as currents move in the earth's magnetic field.

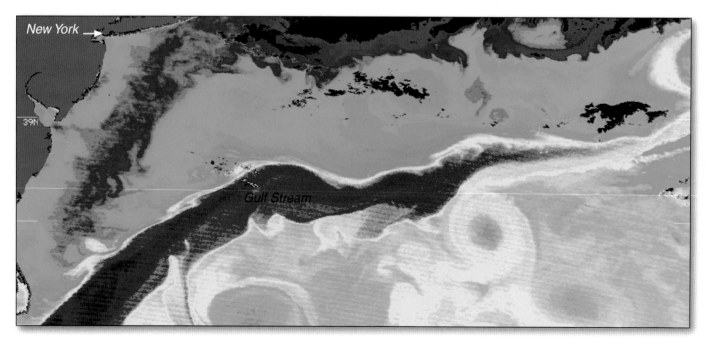

*The path of the Gulf Stream is easily seen off the coast of North America as the dark red in the satellite photo above.
The color red depicts the warmest waters, and the coldest water is depicted in black.*

PATHFINDER OF THE SEAS

Considered the first modern oceanographer, U.S. Navy Lieutenant Matthew Maury wrote The Physical Geography of the Sea, *the first textbook on modern oceanography, in 1855.*

Matthew Fontain Maury was born in 1806 in Virginia. When he was nineteen he fulfilled a boyhood desire by becoming a midshipman. During a recovery from a serious stagecoach accident in 1842, the bedridden Maury read Psalm 8:8 that spoke of "the paths of the seas." Maury believed God's Word and decided to find and chart these movements of ocean waters, or currents, that the Scriptures described.

Recovered from his injuries, he later headed the Navy's Depot of Charts and Instruments and continued his sea path odyssey with vigor. From 1841 to 1853, Maury conducted a systematic study of ocean surface currents. Maury contacted ocean captains and asked that, during their voyages, they drop bottles containing information on where to return them if found. Such messages in bottles were, and still are, important because, unlike a ship that can be affected by both wind and current, sealed bottles are borne by water alone. Maury gave special logbooks to sea captains so they might record information on local currents and winds. He also studied old ships' logs regarding weather, winds, and currents.

By 1847 he had compiled a series of ocean current and wind charts that became popular with merchant marine and naval personnel worldwide. About the same time, Maury perfected a sounding method using nothing more than a lead weight and a very long line. A cautious scientist, he dispelled many errors and myths about the oceans that were accepted at the time.

God had granted his desire to understand Psalm 8:8, for Maury was indeed able to map out the paths of the seas that the Bible described, thereby contributing greatly to marine navigation. In 1853, Maury's industrious efforts were rewarded when he became the American representative at the first international marine conference in Belgium.

The detailed work of Matthew Maury is acknowledged with the following legend found on all pilot charts:

"Founded upon the researches made and the data collected by Lieutenant M.F. Maury, U.S. Navy."

Is it any wonder Maury has been called the Pathfinder of the Seas?

Lieutenant M.F. Maury

Chapter Five
WEATHER

It was to be an exciting 600-mile (960-km) yacht race around a lighthouse off the Irish coast that August of 1979. Sailors of the Fastnet race feared that calm winds would not test their true sailing skills and equipment. Unbeknownst to them, a storm of incredible intensity was brewing. Born west of Lake Michigan on August 10, the day before the race began, the storm sped across the Atlantic toward the Fastnet racecourse. At noon on August 13 the storm suddenly deepened, but due to a series of mistaken, conflicting, and tardy weather readings, the race proceeded. In the inky blackness of night, the "meteorological bomb" blew up among 303 racing yachts containing 2,700 men and women. In one of the worst disasters in yachting history, 15 people perished due to hypothermia or drowning, 5 boats sank, and 24 crews abandoned their vessels. Though some wind gusts reached hurricane force (60-70 mile [96-112 km] per hour), the smashing waves coming from all directions caused the most devastation. Some of those dangerous waves were up to 50 feet (15 m) in height. Only 85 of the 303 yachts made it to the finish line.

How could this disaster have happened? A board of inquiry later determined that the "explosively developing meteorological and oceanographic conditions . . . [were] essentially unpredictable." The "culprits" of this deadly storm were areas of low air pressure in the atmosphere. The storm itself was a unique area of low pressure called a depression. England is used to depression-caused winds and rain in August. However, as this storm moved off the east coast of North America and over the North Atlantic, another low-pressure area sat over the ocean to its north. This low fed the storm cold air and kept it moving right toward the racecourse — a recipe for disaster. The depression's movement actually supplied energy to the high waves experienced by the yachters. Weather forecasters have much to learn regarding the critical meeting of the ocean and atmosphere.

In August 1992, a storm from the coast of central Africa was tracked across the Atlantic. Weather patterns formed that

Damage done by Hurricane Andrew

fed upon each other causing the storm to grow to monstrous proportions. On the 17th of August a name was given to this seething weather pattern — Andrew. Even with sophisticated tracking equipment, monitoring the storm across the tropical Atlantic was difficult. Twice, heavy winds almost disrupted the storm, but it eventually grew stronger. Now a hurricane, Andrew enveloped southern Florida in a roaring intensity difficult to describe. Rains were so heavy that one could hardly tell the division between land and sea; winds howled at gusts up to 177 miles (285 km) per hour. When it was over, twenty-six people had lost their lives and $26 billion of damage was

Hurricane Andrew from space

done. Rescue workers surveying the area said the devastation seemed like a thermonuclear blast. Large portions of the south Florida coast were flattened.

These two destructive examples graphically show the relationship of the oceans to changing weather patterns. The oceans control all large weather patterns on earth. Because of the large surface area, the oceans act as a giant "solar collector," where heat is collected, stored, and released. With such a huge amount of energy (heat) accumulating, is it any wonder that weather patterns sometimes produce hurricanes and cyclones that wreak havoc when they encounter land?

El Niño and La Niña

In July 2002, scientists were puzzled because thousands of two-foot jumbo flying squid (*Dosidicus*) washed up on

the shores of southern California. One marine biologist said she could not understand why what seemed to be perfectly healthy squid were dying. As research continued, the evidence pointed to the phenomenon called "El Niño."

For hundreds of years, Peruvian fishermen noticed that a warm current appeared around Christmas time. They called this warming El Niño which is Spanish for "Christ child." Occasionally the El Niño warming was greater and more persistent than usual. Now known to affect more than just Peru, scientists call this greater change the warm phase of ENSO (El Niño/Southern Oscillation). El Niño is a disruption of normal conditions in the oceans and atmosphere of the tropical Pacific. The usual temperature differences between the surface waters of the east and west Pacific give way to equally warm waters from the equatorial Pacific. This unusually warm condition results in disturbances in the climate worldwide. For example, in the early 1980s a southerly shift in the tropical rain belt caused severe drought in Indonesia and Australia and heavy rains in California. Additionally, the El Niño-caused deepening of warm water off South America prevents the cold, nutrient-rich waters from rising to the surface, killing fish in coastal waters and thereby affecting sea birds and ocean mammals as well. Fortunately, when meteorologists identify even small changes in the atmosphere, they are occasionally able to predict a strong El Niño event more than a year in advance.

Although not as devastating, a contrasting event called La Niña ("the little girl") produces colder-than-normal episodes. This cold phase of ENSO creates strong nutrient upwelling and currents, as well as colder conditions extending from the coast of South America into the central Pacific. The weather patterns responsible for producing a La Niña event are quite complex.

CORIOLIS EFFECT

At the equator, the earth rotates at a rate of approximately 1,000 miles per hour. As the earth turns, it tends to rotate out from under the oceans and "leave them behind," as it were. Since the earth spins to the east, the waters tend to accumulate along western shores of the continents. This effect stems from the Coriolis force, a force produced by the eastward rotation of the earth. This force not only influences the circulation of ocean currents and winds but also affects all moving objects — boats, airplanes, and even a thrown basketball. The Coriolis effect must be considered when plotting ocean currents and wind patterns as well as travel by boat or aircraft. In 1835 the French physicist and mathematician Gaspard de Coriolis first described this phenomenon which causes the winds and currents to be

The arrows in this diagram show the direction of air flow within a hurricane.

deflected either to the left or to the right, depending upon the hemisphere and the speed of motion. It has no effect at the equator, which is why hurricanes do not form there. Furthermore, the Coriolis effect prevents winds blowing directly from high pressure to low pressure. It also influences the direction of ocean currents and accounts for the familiar circulation of airflow around hurricanes.

HURRICANES

In August 1969 the warning went out to Pass Christian, Mississippi, that Hurricane Camille was approaching from the Gulf of Mexico. Storm warnings were issued throughout the area and residents fled to safety farther inland. However, 24 residents of the Richelieu Apartments on U.S. Highway 90 decided to ignore the warnings and hold a popular "hurricane party" during the tempest. The storm approached with an unimaginable fury literally tearing the apartments from their foundations. Twenty-three of the partying residents perished and the one survivor suffered serious injuries.

A hurricane is the most fearsome tropical storm. Hurricanes in the Indian Ocean are called cyclones, and those in the China Sea are called typhoons. Hurricanes form over a warm sea surface and require very high air humidity and a force to start the wind spiraling. The Coriolis effect supplies the force which starts the moisture-laden warm air spinning in a circular or spiral fashion. The winds increase in velocity and intensity over the open sea with no landforms to impede them. A low-pressure, cloud-free center with a diameter of about ten miles is called the "eye" of a hurricane. Heavy rain clouds spiral in toward the eye around which the ascending winds rotate. Hurricanes rarely penetrate far inland since they require huge quantities of moist air and a smooth surface. Meteorologists estimate that for every fifty tropical depressions that form, five of them will become a tropical storm; from those five, two or three hurricanes will develop. Like tornadoes, hurricane winds spiral in a clockwise direction in the Southern Hemisphere and counterclockwise in the Northern, due to the Coriolis effect.

The decreased air pressure that hurricanes cause results in devastating storm surges that flood coastal areas. Nine out of every ten people who die in hurricanes drown due to storm-surge induced flooding. On November 12, 1970, a heavy storm surge caused by a cyclone hit East Pakistan (Bangladesh), taking over 300,000 lives. The effects of storm surges are similar to tsunamis caused by undersea earthquakes;

however, tsunamis, unlike hurricanes, can occur during otherwise good weather.

In contrast, as much damage and loss of life that hurricanes engender, their atmospheric effects are nonetheless beneficial. A hurricane acts as a "safety valve" that distributes hot, humid air which would otherwise make life unbearable in tropical regions. Furthermore, they provide up to 30 percent of the annual rainfall in many parts of the subtropics.

OCEAN TEMPERATURES

Ocean temperatures vary widely in the open ocean, both vertically and horizontally. Icebergs form over frigid waters at either pole, while equatorial waters are quite warm. The nature of water is that it cools and warms more slowly than land does. This is one of the main factors in predicting the world's weather patterns. For example, coastlands influenced by ocean waters will tend to have later and milder seasons than inland (continental) masses.

The surface zone of the ocean, also called the mixed layer, shows little decrease in temperature as the depth increases. Below this surface zone is a layer of sharp temperature difference. This thermocline is a middle layer that ranges from the surface zone down to about 2,600 feet (800 m). Thermoclines may be seasonal or permanent and may change depending on location and water depth. As evaporation occurs, cooling takes place (evaporation is a cooling process). Rapid evaporation causes water to become more salty and dense, contributing to thermocline formation. The colder, salty water is denser, so it sinks. This difference in density explains why warm and cold waters do not easily mix. As you might expect, many animals and almost all plants live in the warm upper layer. Below the thermocline, temperature in the deep zone decreases regularly and rapidly to a point where the temperature stays just above freezing — between 32-37.4°F (0-3°C).

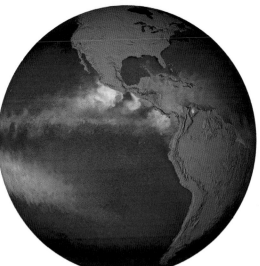

The image above, generated by MODerate-resolution Imaging Spectroradiometer (MODIS), shows by color the differences in the oceans temperatures.

One of the most amazing cold-water survival stories occurred in March 1973. A large Norwegian coal freighter plowed through heavy North Atlantic seas, bound for Scotland. Unfortunately, the 29-man crew underestimated the pounding seas.

Captain Harsem turned the damaged *Norse Variant* back to Norfolk, Virginia, but immense crashing breakers buckled a forward hatch. Soon after that, pounding waves wrecked a forward crane, opening the freighter to the seas. In just seconds, the ship foundered and sank in the angry, frigid waves.

A lone sailor was able to fight the suction of the sinking 20,700-ton freighter and battle to the surface. Twenty-three-year-old Stein Gabrielsen crawled into an empty life raft and began an odyssey in cold-water survival. Sleet, snow and freezing temperatures accompanied 75 mile-an-hour winds. After a huge wave destroyed his raft, Stein found another empty raft nearby. Hypothermia would have killed him had he not put on a windbreaker and life vest before the sinking.

For almost 70 hours Stein held on in the icy North Atlantic, fighting sleepiness and trying to get circulation going in legs numb from cold. An Air Force HC-130 aircraft finally found the young seaman, and dropped two rescue swimmers to his aid. Stein's eyes were swollen and swallowing was difficult, but he could still communicate and soon learned he was the lone survivor of the *Norse Variant's* sinking in the cold North Atlantic.

Chapter Six

HARVESTING THE OCEAN

C an you imagine living and going to school aboard a huge factory fishing ship? Nations such as Russia and Japan have massive self-contained fleets of ships that go to the world's best fishing areas for many months. These large ships have libraries, hospitals, schools, fuel tanks, repair shops and other comforts and necessities for fishermen and their families. These factory ships are used to manage numerous smaller trawlers that daily net huge quantities of fish.

World fish catch per year increased from 20 million tons to more than 90 million tons between 1950 and 1990.

As the world's population continues to climb, many people feel that they must increasingly look to the sea as a source of food, minerals and energy. Waste disposal practices of past decades have affected the fishing industry. Pollutants flushed into the earth's oceans have destroyed once productive fisheries. Polluted and over-fished waters cannot meet what the world needs for the future. Society must learn better management of God's massive yet fragile resource.

Fishing industry

Oceanographers estimate that over 15,300 types of fish inhabit our oceans, some of which are used for food. Fish are an excellent source of protein, making them very nutritious for countless numbers of people. Fishing industries are extremely important because they provide jobs and food for millions. Presently, mainly through ocean fisheries, the ocean supplies about 2 percent of the calories needed by the world population.

Most of the ocean's living creatures are found in the first 600-foot (180 m) depth of the sea. Sardines, tuna, anchovies, mackerel and herring are harvested close to the surface. Pollock, flounder and cod are caught near the ocean floor. The most popular fish caught by the fishing industry in coastal waters are sardines, mackerel, herring, and anchovies.

Over a million tons of herring are caught yearly in the North Pacific and North Atlantic. All told, almost eight out of ten fish caught are used for human consumption. The remainder, such as menhaden and anchovettas, are used for fertilizers, glue, and pet and livestock food.

One-quarter of the world's yearly catch of fish is taken from the Atlantic Ocean, with the North Atlantic being the most productive. The major catches on the once-productive Grand Banks southeast of Newfoundland include lobster and crab. The Pacific Ocean provides over half of the world's catch of fish. The Pacific mackerel, an important resource for fisheries, is found from Japan to Alaska to Chile. The northern Pacific shellfish catch, as defined by the commercial fishing industry, includes mussels, crabs, scallops and oysters.

Trawlermen sort recently caught fish on deck.

A full trawling net of fish has just been brought aboard a fishing boat.

(1,500 m), trawlers trail a massive net sometimes up to a half-mile (0.8 km) behind the boat. Although sizes greatly vary, the opening of some fully extended trawling nets can be almost 250,000 square feet (23,000 square meters). That area is equivalent to five football fields! Stern trawling is not the only trawling method used. Diesel-powered shrimp trawlers off the Gulf Coast of the United States tow their nets from distinctive booms swung out from either side of the boat.

Trawlers capture both open-ocean prey and bottom-dwelling fish or shellfish. Another way to harvest bottom-dwellers instead of using trawling nets

The harvest gathered from the world's oceans gets pulled into boats of all shapes and sizes, from the huge factory ships to one-manned vessels. Fishermen, whether commercial or individual, choose the boat, gear, and fishing method best suited for the number and type of their catch. Gear can include traps, fishing lines with hooks, and many types of nets. The types of nets vary almost as much as the types of boats; among the most popular commercial nets are purse seiners, gill nets, and trawling nets. Fishing techniques usually receive their name by the type of gear used: for example, gill netting, longlining, and purse seining.

Many fishing vessels use the successful stern trawling method to haul and tow over a stern ramp. Sometimes fishing in waters as deep as 4,900 feet

is to drag large steel cages called "dredges" over the ocean floor. These power dredges comb the bottom for shellfish such as clams, scallops, and crabs. Traps, or pots, are also used to capture lobster, crab, and, sometimes, bottom-dwelling fish. In cold and dangerously pitching waters off Alaska's coast, fishing boats lower dozens of these box-like traps, baited with portions of fish, onto the seafloor, while attached signal floats mark their location. Lobster and crab find their way into the traps, but they cannot get out. The boats later return with the brave but fatigued crew to rapidly pull up the traps, remove the angry crustaceans, and then re-bait and drop the trap again — all within minutes. The pay is very good for this intensely dangerous job. High seas, frigid weather, slippery decks, long days, and 700-800-pound pots (when empty) contribute to crabbing's rank as the most dangerous method of commercial fishing, which is historically known to be one of the deadliest occupational fields.

Lobster cage

Traps are used to capture lobster, crab, and bottom-dwelling fish.

nets (each net may be 3 nautical miles [5,500 m] long). The nets form a wall of webbing that entangles the gills of fish such as herring, billfish, and tuna. Squid and shark are also caught. The nets are left to drift all night and up to 100 tons of fish are hauled in by the factory ships the next day. Since dead fish decompose quite rapidly, the catch is processed, packaged (or canned) and quick-frozen right aboard the ship, preventing rotting.

OVERFISHING & BYKILL

In the past, fishing has been so profitable that it has resulted in overfishing — a serious problem that can destroy a fishery. Overfishing does not necessarily mean extinction, but simply that a fish type has been harvested beyond its capability to maintain its population level. As more

Drift net or gill net fishing typically uses the latest technology, including aircraft and electronic detection devices, to find great schools of migrating fish. When located, the fleet of huge factory ships deploys 20 to 50 smaller, faster "catcher boats" that deploy hundreds of miles of drift boats are sent out to catch the fish, population levels of a type of fish may drop, virtually sweeping the area clean. Then, not enough of that kind of fish remains to breed new stock. Flounder, haddock, and cod were popular fishes off New England whose populations reached historic lows. Because of the virtual collapse of the ground-fishing industry in this area, stock recovery measures were enacted in 1995.

Many times, fishing boats catch unwanted fish, or bykill. Such fish caught unintentionally may be anything from delicious red snappers to shark, and they are commonly dumped overboard after they have died. Drift net fishing sometimes catches unintentional creatures such as seals, dolphins, whales, and sea turtles. This technique of fishing has led to protests. In the 1980s, it was estimated that 18 miles (30 km) of these nets were lost each night, left to drift and hopelessly entangle boats and animals alike. In 1993 a moratorium (a temporary suspension agreed upon by various nations) banned the use of these 25-foot (7 m) high nets in international waters, which up until that time, were deployed in enough numbers each night to encircle the planet!

While enjoying the foods God provides, mankind always needs to remember that He also commands us to be stewards, or responsible managers, of the earth and its life.

AQUACULTURE & MARICULTURE

One means of marine stewardship comes through fish farming or aquaculture. This promising technique involves the raising of ocean animals and plants in an aquatic environment under controlled conditions. This important process provides essential animal protein nutrition for scores of people. World aquaculture farms produce millions of tons of shellfish and fish each year. Fish farmers also raise seaweed near ocean shores as well as in ponds, lakes and reservoirs. In Asia especially, farmers cultivate the algae for the carrageenin, algin, and agar that are important food additives.

Due to better technology, many plants and animals are readily harvested from bays, estuaries, and special labs on the seacoast. This method, called mariculture because it takes place in ocean waters, is very much like aquaculture. Japan is the world leader in this process, followed by the United States. An example of mariculture involves the lowly oyster. Every other oyster (about 50 percent) eaten in North America is cultured. This means that young oysters are fastened to mature oyster shells and put into screen bags. The bags are arranged on intertidal mud flats and, after

Anyone who has ever been pounded by surf has experienced the energy of waves.

three years of growth, they are harvested. Another example of this type of stewardship is with the Atlantic salmon. Once an abundant food source, these fish have been threatened by overfishing, as well as damming and pollution. Today salmon are raised successfully by salmon mariculture.

ENERGY

Harvesting the sea includes more than just the life found within its waters. The oceans contain an abundance of non-living resources as well. Think, after all, of its most abundant resource, water. As you sit on the sunny seashore watching the breakers rolling in, think of all the potential energy evident in their power. Even the temperature of the ocean is a potential source of energy! Scientists well over a century ago realized the abundance of energy in the ocean.

Clams are one of the many shellfish raised by fish farmers.

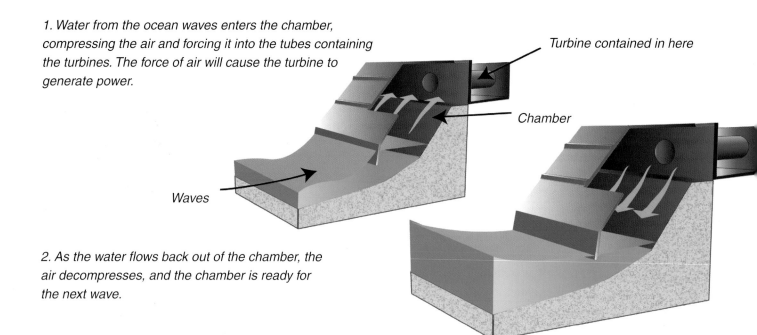

Diagram of a Wave-Energy Plant

1. Water from the ocean waves enters the chamber, compressing the air and forcing it into the tubes containing the turbines. The force of air will cause the turbine to generate power.

Turbine contained in here

Chamber

Waves

2. As the water flows back out of the chamber, the air decompresses, and the chamber is ready for the next wave.

Today, scientists have found that the oceans can solve many of the energy problems that may be encountered in the 21st century. Technology has provided some practical methods for extracting some of the enormous amounts of available energy. The energy sources provided by the ocean are — from lowest to highest energy production — waves, tides, currents, salinity, and thermal gradients.

Anyone who has ever been pounded by surf has experienced the energy of waves. The pounding surf contains enough power to not only push you on a surfboard but also generate energy through wave-energy-conversion power plants. The energy of breaking surf can be compared to a tightly packed line of cars with their throttles revving wide open. Waves have a down and up motion much like a piston, and many wave power generators have been produced to take advantage of this tremendous energy source. Although Sweden, the United States, Norway, and Japan have built wave-power

Tidal power diagram

Outgoing tide

Reversible turbine

plants, their usefulness is offset by the expense of construction and the lack of efficiency.

Tidal power is a form of hydroelectricity produced by harnessing the ebb and flow of tides. The large amount of energy from these tides is used on a limited scale to drive underwater turbines (large machines with rotating parts that produce electricity). Huge barriers containing reversible turbines are built across a gulf or estuary where the range of tides is great. Power plants have already been built in Japan, Algeria, Nova Scotia, Canada, Russia, and the United States. The drawback of such power utilization is that marine plants and animals of the region are affected; concern for the ecosystem accounts for a lack of popularity in using this as a power source.

In 1881, French scientist Jacque D'Arsonval proposed a method called "ocean thermal energy conversion" which uses the ocean's temperature to generate power. Most people are unaware that utilizing thermal gradients (temperature differences) promises the greatest energy production. The gradient between cold deepwater and warm surface water contains enormous potential for the production of energy. The process involves taking advantage of the very low boiling point of liquid ammonia. The ocean's heat is used to boil the ammonia into a pressurized vapor. The vapor is then directed onto a turbine generator to produce electricity. The colder ocean waters are used to condense the ammonia back into a liquid so that it can circulate back through the process again.

Waves produce about two and a half million megawatts of power, but ocean thermal energy conversion can produce ten thousand times more! Unfortunately construction and maintenance costs would be high and the plants would have a low efficiency, requiring massive amounts of cold and warm seawater. The power plants would also need to be located right on the coasts in the tropics where the danger of frequent destructive weather disturbances, such as tropical storms and hurricanes, would interfere.

MINERALS

The ocean abounds with minerals. Did you know that there are about 10 billion tons of gold in the sea? Unfortunately, it is so diluted that it is virtually impossible to recover. Seawater itself contains about fifty quadrillion tons of mineral salts that have been mostly dissolving in the water since the biblical creation week. Major minerals mined from the sea include magnesium, bromine, and, of course, salt! In addition, deposits of zinc, iron and copper are found near jetting undersea hot springs, and small amounts of diamonds are found in some submarine gravel bars.

Billions of tons of strange objects called manganese nodules are scattered over large areas on the floors of the Pacific and Atlantic Oceans. In 1873 the crew of the HMS *Challenger* discovered manganese nodules. Litter from biological processes occurring in surface waters may have something to do with their composition and growth rate. Their average size is about 2.4 inches (6 cm) in diameter, while their average weight is less than half an ounce (12.5 g). Cutting through a nodule reveals layers of iron and manganese oxides along with nickel, copper, and cobalt. Marine scientists think they start to form around a nuclei, such as a bit of bone or shark teeth, much like water forms around a bit of dust in the atmosphere to form a

raindrop. Although the U.S. Bureau of Mines estimates that there are 17.6 billion tons of nodules in the Pacific, it would be dangerous and expensive to extract them from the deep sea floor, as the technology for such an undertaking is as yet undeveloped. Still, one corporation has filed a mining claim on a small portion of the Pacific Ocean even though it will obviously be difficult to travel depths in excess of 12,000 feet (4,000 m) and to avoid hazards such as huge boulders and canyons.

Minerals are not the only physical objects mined from the seas. Gravel, oyster shells, and sand, all used mainly for construction purposes, can be mined from the seafloor. As boring as these rocks might seem, their commercial value is second only to natural gas and oil, which can also be taken from the ocean.

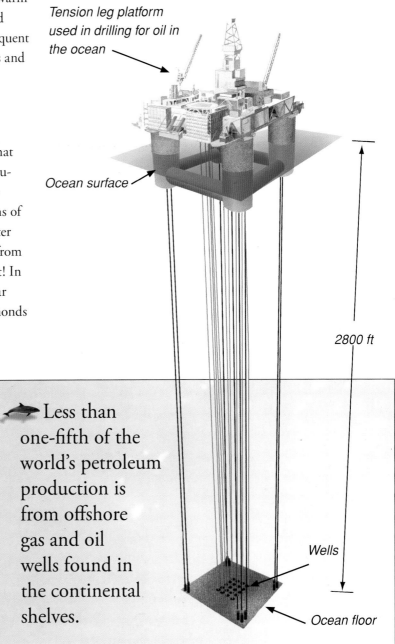

Tension leg platform used in drilling for oil in the ocean

Ocean surface

2800 ft

Less than one-fifth of the world's petroleum production is from offshore gas and oil wells found in the continental shelves.

Wells

Ocean floor

Chapter Seven

MARINE LIFE

Imagine taking a boat out into the ocean on a calm summer night. A bright light suspended into the dark waters will attract invertebrates, various fish, and squid. As animals are drawn to the light, larger predators will be attracted to the growing activity too. Some large fish may feed on smaller squid. The wide variety of plants and animals that God created to fill the oceans defies human comprehension! One trip to an aquarium would grant just a glimpse of the beauty of the underwater world with its abundance of unique life forms especially designed for their particular habitat. This abundant array of life includes not only the swimmers that populate the ocean waters (the *pelagic zone*) but also the creepers, crawlers, and diggers that swarm over the ocean floor (the *benthic zone*). Certainly one would expect to find fish in the seas, but a huge variety of marine animals do not even have backbones. These invertebrates are extremely varied — from arthropods, such as gooseneck barnacles and isopods, to chambered nautiloids and tube worms, to beautiful, undulating nudibranchs and ribbon worms, to sea anemones that bloom like flowers, to colorfully patterned stony coral, to the Portuguese man-of-war and calcareous sponges — all designed and created by God, the Master Designer!

The ocean's water column contains two basic life zones, the *vertical zone* and the *horizontal zone.* The vertical zone, extending from the surface of the sea to the bottom, is

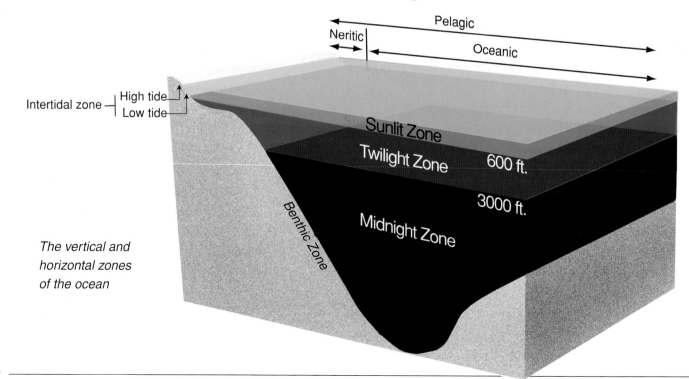

The vertical and horizontal zones of the ocean

divided into three areas by the amount of sunlight reaching each area. The top layer, the *sunlit zone*, extends from the surface to about 600 feet (180 m) below the surface. The sunlight spreading through this zone allows photosynthesis to take place; and, for this reason, most ocean life lives in this region. The second layer, called the *twilight zone*, stretches from 600 to 3,000 feet (180 to 900 m). As depth increases, available light rapidly decreases until there is nothing but the complete darkness of the *midnight zone*. This last layer is not only dark but, at 35.6 to 41°F (2-5°C), is also extremely cold. Life in these last two layers is uniquely fit for its dark, nutrient-poor surroundings.

The horizontal zone is also divided into sections: the *neritic zone*, the area of open water from the low tide mark to the edge of the continental shelf, and the *oceanic zone*, which includes the open sea beyond the continental shelf. Above the neritic zone is a benthic region, the *intertidal zone*, which is the area on the shoreline between low tide and high tide. Tidal pools in the intertidal zone provide an opportunity to see many of God's creatures as they wait for the next refreshing tide to flow in. These varied creatures include brittle stars, periwinkles, acorn barnacles, and hermit crabs, as well as kelp, iridescent red algae, and sea lettuce. Brittle stars belong to an entirely marine animal group. This group includes other sea stars, sea urchins, sea cucumbers, and a curious creature called a "seapig." Like other animal groups, some live only in the neritic zone, some only in the oceanic zone, and some in both.

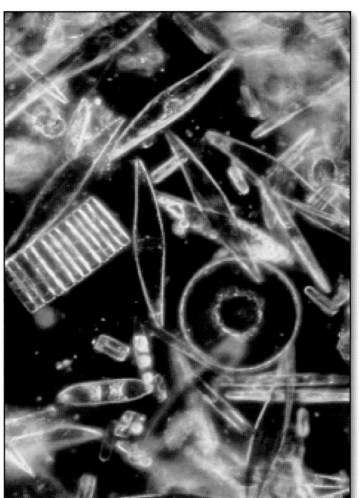

Diatoms

PLANKTON

The general term plankton means, "that which is made to wander," and wander is what these fragile creatures do at the mercy of ocean currents. Plankton are divided into two major groups. Zooplankton (animal plankton) includes various copepods, sea jellies, certain worms, protozoa and mollusks. Phytoplankton (plant plankton) are called autotrophs because they make their own organic nutrients. One of the most abundant phytoplankton are the single-celled diatoms. These algae, most abundant in colder regions, make up more than three-fifths of the plankton in the ocean.

The single-celled protozoa comprise one of the largest populations in the oceans. This huge group includes the beautiful radiolarians and foraminiferans. These tiny, free-floating and diverse organisms, a significant

Satellite imagery of plankton bloom near Newfoundland

chunk of ocean life, form an extensive, but almost invisible layer across the oceans of the world. God created these tiny life forms to inhabit the sunlit areas (the first 600 feet [200 m]) of all the world's oceans. Both radiolarians and planktonic foraminiferans contribute untold trillions of tiny shells and capsules that form a third of the "ooze" found on the deep ocean floor.

Bioluminescence is biologically produced "living light" used by radiolarians and dinoflagellates, an algae member of the plankton. During summer months, dinoflagellates such as *Gonyaulax* or *Noctiluca* ("night shine") release a glowing light when disturbed, such as when a stone is thrown into tropical waters or a hand is drawn through the water. These tiny creatures are not the only living things to use "cool light," so described because it gives off no heat. Types of fish, jellyfish, shrimp, squid, and other sea life also benefit. In the twilight zone, 90 percent of the organisms use bioluminescence to communicate, attract mates or prey, avoid or warn about lurking predators, or simply to say, "Stay away."

"Stay away" is how many people react when they hear of a red tide. Neither the color red, nor tidal actions have anything to do with this phenomenon. For unclear reasons, dinoflagellates suddenly exceed their normal population growth rate and subsequently turn up to 1,000 square miles (2,600 sq. km.) of ocean waters a brownish color. Conditions that oceanographers believe may furnish a red tide event include good light, nutrients, and warm surface temperatures. Many red tides are harmless, but others kill large numbers of fish that later wash ashore — an undesirable

occurrence for beachfront property owners. Poisons from different red tides may accumulate in the tissues of scallops, oysters, and clams, making them poisonous to humans. People who eat these shellfish become quite ill and suffer from nausea, diarrhea, and vomiting. Unfortunately, this paralytic shellfish poisoning is becoming more common throughout the world.

Phytoplankton are at the base of the food web, a complex series of food chains in which animals and plants are connected by their food relationships. Any one species of ocean life can be represented in many different food chains, and every creature in the ocean is a member of a food chain. Author N. J. Berrill gives an example of an oceanic food chain, using a massive humpback whale at the top, and diatoms at the base, or foundation. A ton of herring (about 5,000 fish) would comfortably fill the whale's stomach. Six thousand small copepods (aquatic crustaceans) would fill each fish, and 120,000 diatoms would fill each crustacean! This means that 3.6 trillion diatoms would be needed to fill the stomach of the humpback whale. It is easy to see why some people call this a food pyramid. Can you think of a similar marine food chain or pyramid where people are the consumers at the top?

ALGAE

In Psalm 104:25-27, the Psalmist states that all the creatures in the great and wide sea wait upon their Creator that He may give them their meat in due season. Passages in Genesis make it clear that plants were meat (food) for many animals. The plants of the ocean include the vast group of algae, which supply "meat" for many ocean animals.

The four major types of algae are named by color.

Oceanic food pyramid

Humpback whale

Herring

Crustaceans

Plankton

Giant kelp forest

Almost all of marine brown algae are found along the shores of temperate zones. Some brown algae, called "giant bull kelp," may grow over 200 feet (61 m) long. This kelp, one of the world's fastest-growing plants, forms large underwater forests in the sea. Near Japan and Southern California, specially designed "mower" ships utilize large metal cutting shears under the surface to crop the tops off kelp, while a moving ramp brings the harvest aboard. Another form of brown kelp, sargassum, grows in large areas of the Atlantic near Florida. The brown algae in this area (called the Sargasso Sea) provide food and protection for innumerable animals. A most important commercial product from brown algae is a slimy extract called "algin" that is used in making printer ink and paint, and is used as a thickening agent in foods such as cream pies, mayonnaise, instant pudding, and ice cream.

The most diverse group of algae is the green algae. The beautiful single-celled desmids are one kind of green algae that form a large part of ocean plankton. Green algae grow along seashores, attaching themselves to a rocky foundation and forming wide mats. One common type of green algae is called "sea lettuce."

Plants constantly provide nutrients and water to their cells. Trees and many other plants transport their food and water through special conducting tissues called "xylem" and "phloem." Though lacking in this conductive tissue, algae, like green plants, do have the important pigment called chlorophyll designed by the Creator to capture sunlight and turn it into organic molecules such as sugar. Such a process, called "photosynthesis," is so complex that only God could have designed it!

CRUSTACEANS

Crustaceans are a specific type, or class, of arthropod with paired, jointed appendages and an exoskeleton that is shed periodically. Some people call crustaceans shellfish, but this is incorrect — they do not have real shells, nor are they fish! The 50,000-or-more species of crustaceans range from the tiny daphnia to larger shrimp, crayfish, lobster, and crab.

The immature (younger) stages of crustaceans are a delight to study as they develop in a small aquarium. Barnacles are marine crustaceans, too. The immature barnacles, called "ciprids," are free swimmers. When they reach a

Yellow algae may be the most abundant form of life on this planet. One member of the yellow algae, the diatoms, form part of the critical foundation of the ocean's food chain. The beautiful glass or silica shells that diatoms produce collect on the ocean bottom by the trillions and are scooped up to make freshwater filters, explosives and abrasives. A great area of diatomaceous earth found in California was probably formed during the Genesis flood.

Red algae are found along rocky coasts of subtropical seas. One large group grows along with corals and helps to strengthen the reef. These plants are important in microbiology as a source of agar, a growth medium for colonies of bacteria placed in petri dishes of laboratories. Red algae also have a host of other uses, such as acting as paint binders and food additives.

The largest bivalve, the giant clam, can weigh over 500 pounds (225 kg) and is found in the Pacific and Indian Oceans.

long, krill are found throughout the world's oceans. The cold waters of the Antarctic seas, unlike warmer, tropical waters, are rich in nutrients. These waters contain large numbers of diatoms, which, in turn, are food for the krill. Antarctic animals such as squid, penguins, petrels (a seabird), and whalebone whales gobble up these small, red crustaceans. Krill are a vital part of the ocean's food web. If the krill population suddenly decreased, what might happen to the other "links" in the food web?

MOLLUSKS

There are at least 100,000 species of mollusks, making them one of the largest of all animal phyla. Filter feeders, which include the cockle, clam, scallop, mussel, and oyster, comprise one of the more common groups of mollusks, the "bivalves." A bivalve is easy to identify, because the animal has a two-part, usually symmetrical, shell.

One enemy of scallops and oysters is the sea star. A large bed of oysters can be decimated by a horde of sea stars.

Some bivalves called "pearl oysters" produce beautiful pearls. The formation of a pearl begins when an irritating bit of sand gets inside the oyster. The annoyed oyster responds by slowly secreting layer after layer of shell around the grain of sand. After months a beautiful

certain age, they fasten themselves to a hard surface, usually in an intertidal zone, and begin making their hard shell. Adult barnacles live on their heads all their lives. Their "cirri" or legs are beautiful feather-like appendages designed by the Creator to sweep the water for food particles that are then brought through the shell opening to their mouths. Besides living in intertidal zones, barnacles also hitch a free ride by attaching themselves to things such as whales or the hulls of ships. Because they interrupt the flow of water past the sleek hull of a ship, barnacles increase drag and slow the ship down. Therefore, barnacles must be periodically scraped off.

Norwegian whalers assigned the name "krill" to a type of small, lobster-like crustacean. About two inches

Krill

48

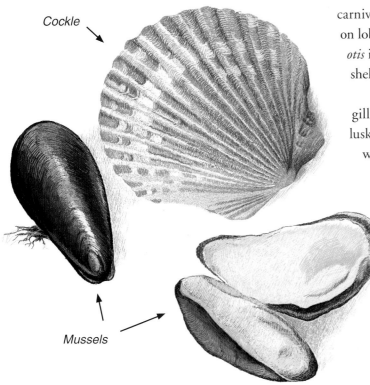

Cockle

Mussels

abalone, conch, limpet, sea slug and periwinkle. Whelks are carnivores and scavengers in temperate waters where they feed on lobsters, crab, and shellfish. The beautiful sea snail *Haliotis* is a large abalone that has a mother-of-pearl ear-shaped shell.

What has three hearts, blue blood and breathes with gills? The answer is the incredible octopus, a shell-less mollusk called a "cephalopod." The octopus was given a name which means "eight feet" because of the eight arms that surround its mouth. Each arm has a single or double-row of strong suction cups. Behind the beaked head is a sac-like body containing the internal organs. Octopuses (or octopi) vary in size. Some may have an arm span of 16 feet (4.8 m), while others are just 1 inch (3 cm) across. The 289 different kinds of octopus are found the world over at great depths or in shallow water. As a food, they are a delicacy in Latin America, Southeast Asia, and the Mediterranean region.

God gave the octopus several unusual defense mechanisms. The octopus is able to alter the outline and form of its body and is known to "ooze" through a crack on a fishing boat and plop overboard back into its watery world. The only condition is that the crack must

pearl may form. Many are deformed and only the best are saved for jewelers. Because the demand for pearls is so high, workers on aquaculture farms grow cultured pearls by purposely injecting oysters with sand grains.

Tiny "univalves" leave miniature bubbles and holes on the shoreline as they quickly dig their way into the protecting sand when a wave leaves them behind. These gastropods ("stomach-footed mollusks") are called univalves because of their one-piece shell, a shell that is often coiled in a beautiful spiral. The conveyor-like tongue of these snails has 3,000 tiny teeth that the mollusks use for scraping algae and drilling holes in other shells. The more common marine gastropods include the larger whelk with its thick, spiral shell as well as

The octopus is the most intelligent of the mollusks. Some learn simple tasks such as opening a jar and others are said to be able to recognize divers.

In March 2002, scientists identified a rare species of giant octopus caught earlier off the coast of New Zealand at a depth greater than 3,000 feet (900 m). When alive, it may have measured almost 13 feet (4 m) long!

A single shark can go through thousands of teeth in a lifetime. During active feeding periods, nurse sharks replace all their front-row teeth every ten to fourteen days.

be as big as their neck. When feeding or alarmed, they can also change color to camouflage themselves or eject a black pigment called "sepia." This ejected cloudy "ink" covers their escape route. Some octopuses possess a sting deadly enough to kill humans.

Squid are also cephalopod mollusks without a shell. A majority of these creatures are open ocean types, although a few live in coastal waters. Eight arms and two much-longer tentacles stretch forward from

around the head of these streamlined animals. Sudden contraction (squeezing) of the mantle cavity sends out a blast of water that can be directed forward or backward by a moveable funnel that enables some of these creatures to move quite rapidly. God designed the squid with side fins for stability and a beak, arms and tentacles to capture prey. All squid effectively grab fish with the hooks or saw-like rings found on the suckers of their arms and tentacles. The greatest quantity of squid is harvested in Japan where the demand for this tasty delicacy is high.

Like an octopus, a squid is a cephalopod with eight arms, but the squid has two longer tentacles bringing the number of apendages to ten.

Fish

The more than 20,000 species of fish (phylum Chordata) are divided into two superclasses: those without jaws and those with jaws. The fish with jaws are further divided into "cartilaginous" fish and "bony" fish.

Not only do jawless fish not have jaws, but they also do not have pairs of pelvic and pectoral fins, either. Hagfish and lampreys are examples of jawless fish. The scavenging hagfish are famous for coating their bodies with thick slime when disturbed. The parasitic American sea lampreys became infamous by invading the Great Lakes and devastating the lake trout and other sport fish populations.

Cartilaginous fish consist of over 1,000 species of rays, sharks, and chimaeras. These fish have a skeleton composed of cartilage, which is the same substance that provides the shape to the human nose and ears.

Belonging to the most widespread class of vertebrates, bony fish make up about 95 percent of all the known

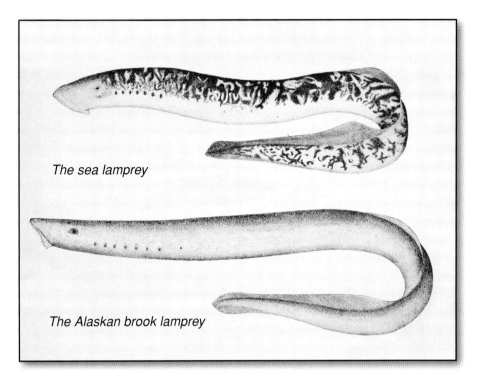

The sea lamprey

The Alaskan brook lamprey

types of fish. As the name indicates, all bony fish have a bony skeleton. They are divided into two main groups, ray-finned fish (e.g. tuna, bass) and fleshy-finned fish (e.g. lungfish and lobefin). Bony fish are incredibly diversified; consider the differences between the sea horse, eel, and tuna.

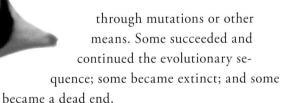

Evolutionists have long claimed that the fossil-containing rocks record the path that evolution took in producing the many types of animals that currently exist. They claim that one type of animal produced other types through mutations or other means. Some succeeded and continued the evolutionary sequence; some became extinct; and some became a dead end.

If, however, such a story were true and the fossil record was recorded over millions of years, then fossil hunters should find millions of animals showing the transitions between one kind and another. What has been found? Fossilized rays and sharks that are clearly identifiable as rays and sharks — just as God created them. They are not peculiar creatures in an evolutionary stage on their way to becoming something else. The fossil record shows fish to have always been fish. They did not evolve

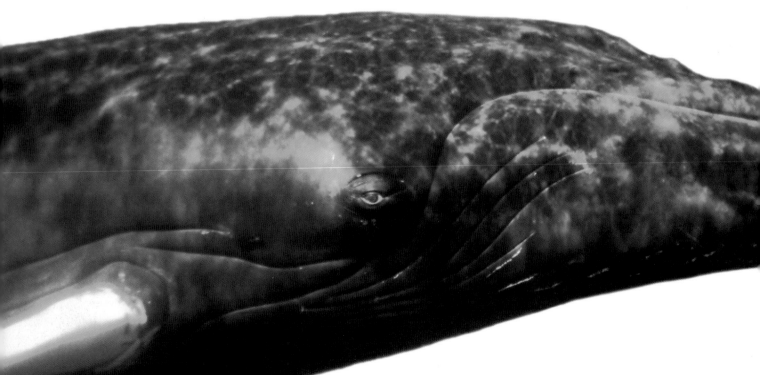

from invertebrates (animals without a backbone like a sea star), nor did they evolve into amphibians (animals that begin life in water with gills but later have lungs and breathe air).

have only one blowhole. These animals also form social groups called "pods" which migrate thousands of miles to special breeding grounds.

AQUATIC MAMMALS

Although their bodies have a fishlike shape and they spend their entire lives in water, whales are not fish. Since they breathe air, have some hair, and give birth to live young, whales are mammals. God gave these big, graceful creatures tail flukes (horizontal, flat fins) that enable them to wiggle up and down, rather than side-to-side like fish, as they swim. Whales must come to the surface to breathe; when they do, they expel air through a dorsal blowhole and and in the process sometimes spout water high into the air. Two types of whales, baleen whales and toothed whales, roam the world's oceans. Ninety percent of the whales, including sperm whales, dolphins, porpoises, orcas, belugas, and beaked whales, belong to the latter group. Besides having teeth, toothed whales also

WHALE AND DOLPHIN COMMUNICATION

Toothed whales use "echolocation," a type of underwater radar, to search for their food. Their use of sharp clicks and other sounds is the biological equivalent to sonar. Both sonar and echolocation involve the production of sound waves that reflect, or bounce off, an object and return to the sender. The sound waves can travel through air (the method used by bats) or water (the method used by dolphins, whales, and submarines). Biologists believe that toothed whales, can also use echolocation to stun or kill smaller fish. The evolution theory says such an amazing scheme came about by mutations and natural selection. Scientific observation, however, does not support this. Years of observation only reveal that living things have the ability to be quite adaptable within the boundaries given to them at creation. Only the all-wise Creator of the Bible could design such an incredible search-and-navigation system!

Like other toothed whales, dolphins have excellent echolocation systems and unique communication skills. These gregarious mammals communicate in a number of ways, based on different circumstances. They commonly slap the water's surface with their flukes. They also use a complex series of clicks and whistles that travel for long distances underwater. When in distress, they use several distinct calls. Such communication is called "phonation."

ARE THERE ANY NEW SPECIES OF OCEAN LIFE TO BE FOUND?

Although it may seem like biologists have found just about all life forms of the deep, the opposite is probably true. There may be many, many species of animals and plants yet to be found in the world's oceans! Indeed, the number of species of ocean fish is anywhere from 15,000 to well over 40,000. Only God knows the total number, of course. Biologists have found many of the known animals and plants simply because they were hard to miss due to their size, number or locality. Rare surprises still lurk. Scientists continue to find "weird and wonderful animals" in the deeper parts of the oceans. The ocean is still unknown territory with surprising new discoveries just waiting to be made.

"PREHISTORIC" SPECIES OF THE OCEANS

Some life forms seem so strange-looking that it would be tempting to call them "prehistoric." One example of a "living fossil" is the coelacanth, or lobefin fish, thought to be extinct for "80 million years" until one was caught alive off the east African coast in 1938! In 1997, another population of these fish was found in Indonesia as well. Finding populations of "living fossils" comes as no surprise to creation scientists who would expect such findings because they maintain that the earth is not as old as evolutionists propose.

Ocean "monsters" – myths?

Through the centuries, man has encountered unusual creatures that defy explanation. Some of these sea "monsters" have found their places in many a "fish tale."

Mammoths of the deep sea, the giant-sized squid, with their slimy tentacles and arms, sharp beaks, and massive size, could well be called monsters. Jules Verne thought so as he recounted an exciting attack by a giant squid (*Architeuthis dux*) in his classic book, *20,000 Leagues under the Sea*. Giant squid are known mainly by the fearsome sucker-marks left on

sea squid called the "colossal squid" (*Mesonychoteuthis*). The beaks and mantles of these rare large invertebrates have been found in the stomachs of whales, but only a few whole specimens have been found. So, it remains to be seen if the adults reach their estimated size.

Giant-sized squid are not the only marine life to cause shivers. Many people shudder at the sight of a snake on land. So, to have a snake swim up next to them could make them react as if they had seen a monster. Sea snakes

Coelacanth

the skin of whales, parts of their huge arms in whale stomachs, and those squid bodies that have been washed ashore or caught in fishermen's nets. Several species of these deep sea giants are known to exist. However, observing adult ones alive remains tantalizingly out of reach due to their deep-sea habitat. After examining over 105 giant squid, a New Zealand scientist corrected one myth about the *Architeuthis* — its size is often less than reported. None of the 105 exceeded a total length of 43 feet (13 m). Long regarded as the largest, the giant squid may have to hand that title over to an Antarctic deep-

The 10-15 inch (25-38 cm) wide eyes of the giant squid are the largest in the animal kingdom. However, colossal squid eyes may be larger. On April 4, 2003, a colossal squid believed to be a juvenile was found with an eye measuring 12 inches (30 cm) in diameter.

swim well but have difficulty getting about on land due to their paddle-like tails. These marine reptiles consist of at least 50 species found mostly in the western Pacific and Indian Oceans. Sea snakes have extremely potent venom; yet, due to the way they bite, only a fraction of their bites kill. These snakes are also non-aggressive so people are not known to receive sea snake bites while swimming in the water. Most of the fatalities are local fishermen who grab or step on a sea snake caught in their net.

Fanfin anglerfish

Sea snake

The deep ocean bottom has by far the world's strangest creatures — some with large mouths and others with huge, bulging eyes. Such deep-sea creatures include the 7-inch (18 cm) long blackdevil anglerfish, complete with a bioluminescent lure that sticks out to attract attention. The big-eyed longspine channel rockfish can be found resting comfortably at an amazing 5,764 feet (1,757 m) on the ocean bottom. The massive pelican-like mouth of the 5-foot (1.6 m) long deep-sea gulper eel dominates its sac-like body — a body whose whip-like tail ends with a glowing tip!

Blackdevil anglerfish

Chapter Eight

EXPLORING THE CORAL REEF

Coral reefs may be defined as limestone formations rich in marine life in tropical waters. These reefs are distributed throughout the world, mainly in equatorial regions. Coral reefs may be made up of more than five hundred species of tiny animals, such as stony corals, packed into dense colonies.

Lettuce coral, soft coral, sea fan coral, and mushroom coral are among the different types of coral that God created. Corals are tiny marine invertebrates that consist of a tubular body, a mouth, and tentacles covered with venomous stinging cells which are used to snare tiny floating plankton. Water warmer than 70°F (21°C) and significant light penetration are essential for those coral that also get food from photosynthetic algae living inside of them. Friendly currents supply

life-giving oxygen as well as the carbonate and calcium ions needed for reef building. The reef grows as the corals join together to form colonies. Branches and successive layers are formed by budding and by the addition of new members which swim freely before attaching themselves. After attaching, the corals will secrete a new external skeleton over the old one.

Congregations of the reef-building corals with their limestone skeletons form vast reefs and islands. Life in a typical coral reef is a rich diversity of lobed corals, sponges, barber pole shrimp, cobalt sea stars, moray eels, sea urchins, cleaner fish, sea fans, clown fish, butterfly fish, sea anemones, and much more. This ocean life in its clear, warm waters draws local inhabitants and tourists who view the wonders through their snorkeling masks.

Sadly, a phenomenon called "coral bleaching" has devastated wide areas of once beautiful coral reefs, including the Florida Keys and the eastern Pacific. Coral bleaching first came to public notice in 1963 after Jamaican corals suffered from flooding during Hurricane Flora. Bleaching occurs when corals containing photosynthetic algae get rid of the algae. Since the algae supplies color as well as nutrients, the coral becomes whiter and may die. Although what happens during bleaching is known, no one is sure of the exact cause of this disease. The culprit named by most is warmer-than-normal sea temperature. The worst and most widespread bleaching on record occurred in 1998 when 23 reefs experienced bleaching. Massive bleaching in the Great Barrier Reef in 2002 made that the second worst year. As the phenomenon continues to be studied, scientists hope to document not only how quickly coral regrowth occurs but also how future bleaching can be lessened.

TYPES OF REEFS

There are three types of coral reefs: *atolls* that are circular reefs enclosing a lagoon; *barrier reefs* that are separated from the shore by a deep, wide lagoon; and *fringing reefs* that are platforms of living coral.

Most atolls are found in the Pacific Ocean. Micronesia, a chain of islands in the Pacific, has 134. Atolls formed over sinking, inactive volcanoes and are surrounded by the open sea. The process of atoll formation began when coral growth on underwater slopes continued as the volcano sank. On many atolls, as soil lodged on the exposed reef, tropical plants like mangroves took root, attracting beautiful birds and forming a gorgeous coral island. This type of tropical island is typically seen in Internet ads and travel posters.

Fringing reefs have a volcanic island in the center of an underwater outer margin made up of coral rock and living coral. Fringing reefs can be found in the Hawaiian Islands.

Shoals are very much like reefs because they are a submerged ridge or bar covered by sand or mud, near enough to the water's surface to be a hazard to ships. In May of 1849 the United States issued Patent 6449 for a device that would float vessels over dangerous shoals by means of inflatable cylinders. The inventor? Abraham Lincoln!

Formation of an Atoll

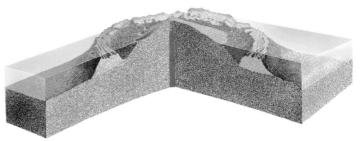

1. Since the Genesis flood's conclusion, the ocean crust has been cooling. As it cools, its density increases, causing the crust — and any inactive oceanic volcanoes sitting on it — to sink slightly relative to the continents. Many atolls may have developed due to this process.

2. Fringing coral growth begun before the sinking would continue to grow up from the underwater slopes of the volcanoes.

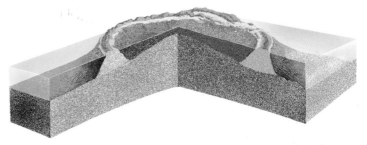

3. As soil became lodged in the exposed reef, tropical plants took root, creating small islands.

Clown fish

Aerial view of the Great Barrier Reef

CORAL REEFS & MANGROVES

Mangrove trees form an important part of a healthy coral reef. These large, tropical trees are found in saltwater wetlands of tropical and sub-tropical Africa, Asia, and the southwest Pacific. God designed mangroves to thrive in brackish water on muddy tidal flats. Their tangled, twisting prop roots anchor on the shores and collect sediment and debris — just the place for other island vegetation to grow. Smaller roots designed with air passages and breathing pores conduct oxygen from the air to plant tissues underwater. Mangrove roots provide clear water for the coral by trapping sediment and clean water by filtering land runoff and removing pollutants. The trees also protect the shoreline (and thus the coral reefs) from erosion by storm waves.

Mangrove fruit is a reddish-brown berry with a single seed. In an unusual fashion, it germinates inside the fruit still attached to the parent tree, forming a root that rapidly anchors the seedling in the rich mud. This growth pattern produces mangrove thickets, which provide a nursery for many coral-reef fish and a habitat for shrimp, crabs, and other fish.

GREAT BARRIER REEF

The Great Barrier Reef, "the largest biological construction on the planet," is an extensive coral reef ecosystem. Comprised of a series of coral formations and small islands in the Coral Sea along the northeastern

Mangrove tree

coast of Australia, the reef system extends some 1,429 miles (2,300 km) down the coast of Queensland. Many different types of reefs, including true barrier reefs, make up the Great Barrier Reef. In the north, the reefs hug the shore; yet, in the southern sections, many lie more than 60 miles (100 km) from the mainland. The lagoon between the reefs and the mainland varies from very shallow and narrow in the north to very wide with water passages deep enough for ocean liners in the south. The Great Barrier Reef and its waters attract much wildlife. Seabirds and green turtles use various reef islands as breeding grounds, over 1,500 species of fish swarm through the waters, and the reefs themselves consist of approximately 400 species of beautiful yellow, red, purple, and green coral polyps. Unfortunately, these radiant polyps have been attacked since the 1960s by the voracious crown-of-thorns sea stars. Biologists have not determined what caused the outbreak of this ongoing problem. The reef is now a national park, protected by the Great Barrier Reef Marine Park Authority.

The Great Barrier Reef consists of several layers of reef growth. Evolutionists claim that the base of the reef is approximately "600,000 years old" and that the most recent reef growth began "eight thousand or more" years ago. Although the term *uniformitarianism* is usually used only in geology, the idea behind it can also be found in biological dating methods. The standard way of measuring coral reef age is by measuring the current growth rate of coral and applying that rate to the reef thickness. The problem with that method is the assumption that corals grow at a steady rate — the rate measured now at the surface. However, studies indicate that corals can grow faster than the rate

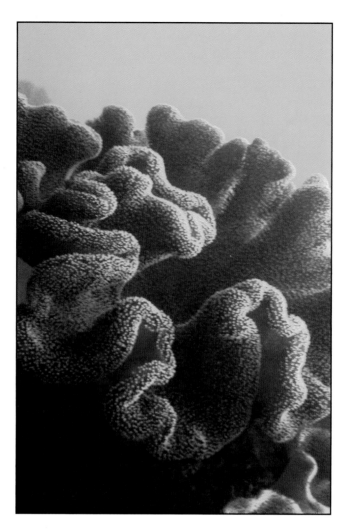

Purple Polyps

*Coral Rockcod
(above)*

usually given. In 1997, scientists measured growing corals in the Great Barrier Reef. The tips of the corals studied grew about 5 inches (13 cm) per year. If this growth were all vertical (which it was not), it would equal a vertical growth rate of approximately 1,493 feet (455 m) in 3,500 years. If the Great Barrier Reef is 260 to 460 feet (80-140 m) thick, then only a quarter of the growth needs to be in the vertical direction for the reef to have grown to its present size in the last 3,500 years. This would fit right in to the end of the Ice Age according to the biblical timescale. Therefore, this massive reef of limestone and coral could have easily formed within the biblical timeframe of thousands of years!

Chapter Nine

OCEANIC VESSELS

National Oceanic and Atmospheric Administration research ship

Among all these are the explorers, who can be serious researchers or simply those yearning to roam the boundless expanse of the ocean. Whatever their purpose, every vessel must be ready to meet the ocean's demanding requirements; and every sailor must be ready to navigate this unmarked liquid highway.

MODERN OCEANOGRAPHIC RESEARCH SHIPS

Scientists gather information regarding the behavior of the seas by using a variety of tools. These include satellites used in conjunction with the latest computer technology to show current patterns of the seas as well as water-surface temperature. Ocean buoys transmit data they have gathered to satellites, which then transfer the data to either shore bases or oceanographic research vessels.

Vessels of all shapes, sizes, and materials keep the world's liquid highway busy. These include anything from rafts to specially designed research ships and submarines. Some travel for pleasure, others for work. Some carry passengers or cargo, while others transport the world's navies.

The most important tool of the oceanographer is the oceanographic research ship. The flexible capabilities of these hardy ships are designed for long, detailed voyages. Research ships often carry a crew of thirty-five or more scientists who will stay at sea for months. Wet and dry laboratories are used for analyzing and studying specimens. Libraries with satellite connections to large databases on shore are also essential. Even the propulsion is unique. Variable-pitch propellers use steam turbine or diesel electric engines designed for very low as well as

Coast Guard vessel

very high speeds. Oceanographic ships may also have fixed bow thrusters for greater maneuverability at slow speeds. The ship can also be kept virtually stationary in a current if necessary.

Oceanographic research ships, which are really ocean-going working platforms, contain very expensive equipment such as radar, satellite tracking gear, helicopter landing pads, deep sea vehicles, heavy cranes, and winches capable of holding over nine miles (14,500 m) of wire cable. They also have bathythermographs for continuous temperature readings and PDR (precision depth recorders) to accurately determine the depth of the ocean. An oceanographic research ship would not be complete without the standard Nansen bottles designed to measure temperatures and collect water samples at specific depths. Other oceanographic instruments include underwater video cameras, STD (salinity/temperature/depth) sensors and current meters. Research ships even have powder magazines for underwater explosion studies to measure reflected sound waves.

The deep sea drilling ship *Glomar Challenger* made marine science history after successfully completing an important drilling program of 1,092 holes at 624 sites throughout the world's oceans. Computers were used to maintain the ship's position, as samples — sometimes a mile (1.7 km) long — were taken. *Glomar Challenger* extracted 60 miles (97 km) of cores from the ocean before being retired in 1983.

SUBMARINES AND SUBMERSIBLE VEHICLES

Surface ships and divers using scuba gear can investigate only a fraction of the ocean. In order to probe the depths, a diving bell or submarine of some sort is needed. In the 1930s, two men, Beebe and Barton, used the first bathysphere, a hollow steel ball lowered by a cable. They reached their greatest depth of 3,028 feet (923 m) in 1934. Over a decade later, famous explorer and scientist Auguste Piccard built a vessel called the bathyscaph that could go down and up from the chilly depths freely without bulky and troublesome cables.

Submersibles, the sophisticated research submarines used currently by oceanographers and engineers, enter and observe the ocean waters with almost no disturbance. Dozens of these submersibles explore virtually every part of this strange, wonderful marine world. Technology has provided these vehicles with coring devices, mechanical arms, video cameras, and sonar. Most deep sea cameras are built to operate at depths ranging from 600 feet (183 m) to 9,842 feet (3,000 m). Two cameras have been tested at a depth close to 7

The first bathysphere was a hollow steel ball lowered by a cable.

miles (11,000 m). The four basic kinds of submersibles include bathyscaphs, mid-water drifters, submarines, and rescue vehicles.

One of the more fascinating submersibles was the 50-foot (15 m) mid-water drifter *Ben Franklin*. It was designed by Jacques Piccard to literally drift within the Gulf Stream! In July 1969, six scientists embarked on a month-long voyage of observing physical conditions of this great stream of water. From the beginning, the team of researchers made amazing discoveries, from an unexpected lack of marine life where they drifted to encountering stronger currents and eddies than anticipated.

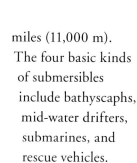

In 1960, Lt. Don Walsh and Jacques Piccard achieved depths of nearly seven miles (10.9 km) in the Swiss-designed bathyscaph *Trieste*.

Since the thawing of the Cold War, some American nuclear submarines, once used for military and security purposes, have been used by scientific staff as ideal platforms to undergo oceanographic investigations. In 1996, one sturgeon-class submarine hosted a science group that resulted in the placing of long-term observation buoys and gathering of over 1,500 water samples. These nuclear submarines, however, cannot descend as deep as research submarines that plunge to maximum depths of just over 3,000 feet (915 m). ROVs (remotely operated vehicles) deployed from these submarines reach a depth of 9,800 feet (2,987 m).

Nuclear submarine USS Florida

Only since the mid-1970s has it become economical and practical to operate deep sea vehicles such as DSVs (deep submergence vehicles) and the unmanned vehicles called ROVs. Some ROVs are designed to crawl along the dark seafloor with lights and a video recorder while attached to the mother ship by cable and power cord. Other ROVs have several thrusters that can keep the unit hovering above the seafloor or have it prowling narrow passageways of sunken ships. Some deep-diving chambers move up and down by dropping and adding ballast, but they have no capacity to move horizontally. U.S. Navy nuclear submarines carry deep submergence rescue vehicles (DSRVs) which are designed to rescue crews of disabled submarines. The depth limit for these is 5,000 feet (1,524 m) — almost a mile.

How can all that heavy steel float?

The aircraft carrier USS *Abraham Lincoln* is like an immense floating city with food, housing, and equipment to support over five thousand crew members. How can all that accumulated weight stay afloat? Although metal ships have been built for almost two centuries, the answer to the buoyancy question has been around much longer.

Archimedes, a Greek physicist, inventor, and mathematician, founded the science of "hydrostatics," the study of liquids and pressure. The associated Archimedes principle states that the force holding up an object partially or totally immersed in a fluid equals the weight of the fluid that the object pushes out of the way. In other words, a ship like a huge aircraft carrier actually does sink — until it displaces an amount of water equal in weight to the weight of the aircraft carrier. The weight must be distributed over a wide area to be effective. This explains both the buoyancy of ships and boats (including submarines) and the apparent loss of weight of objects underwater. An object's weight pulls downward in the direction of gravity. Pressure from the water's buoyant force pushes upward. These opposing forces counteract each other, giving objects an apparent weight-loss. NASA uses this principle to prepare their astronauts for the weightlessness of space. They have the astronauts work on parts of the space shuttle submerged in water tanks 25 feet (7.6 m) deep.

Why does a submarine not sink to the bottom of the ocean and stay there?

Submarines are boats designed to stay submerged for a prolonged period — anywhere from a few minutes to several months. Submarines have special tanks along each side called ballast tanks that hold either air or water. The submarine submerges by flooding its ballast tanks to lose its positive buoyancy and reach neutral buoyancy; this means that it displaces its own weight of water. Subs dive by using movable horizontal rudders called diving planes. Depending on how full the tanks are filled with water, the submarine will sink to a predetermined depth. Los Angeles class military submarines operate at depths of about 1,475 feet (450 m). When the captain signals for the submarine to surface, compressed air forces the water out of the ballast tanks, making the boat lighter than the surrounding water, or positively buoyant. The diving planes are angled upwards, bringing the boat to the surface. Today submarines are streamlined boats having a double hull. The inner hull is called the pressure hull, with ballast and fuel tanks between it and the outer hull.

HOW

DID PEOPLE IN EARLY HISTORY CROSS THE OCEAN?

Through the centuries sailors used a variety of instruments to find their way across the waves. How do you suppose sailors found their way during the day when there was nothing but sea all around? Everything looked the same — how could they be sure they were not sailing in a huge circle?

One answer was the sun. It always rises in the east and sets in the west. On a ship heading west, the captain and his mates made sure the sun was at their backs in the morning and dead ahead in the afternoon. At night of course, they had the stars to steer by. At different times of the year, different constellations would be in the night sky. Experienced sailors knew where the North Star and other critical navigational stars were located. Of course, if the sky was overcast, or the ship was caught in a storm, these heavenly directional tools were useless. (Read the 27th chapter of the Book of Acts for a thrilling sea voyage with the apostle Paul on the stormy Mediterranean Sea.) Through the centuries, special instruments were invented to take some of the guesswork out of this process of navigation (*navis* means "ship" and *agere* means "to direct").

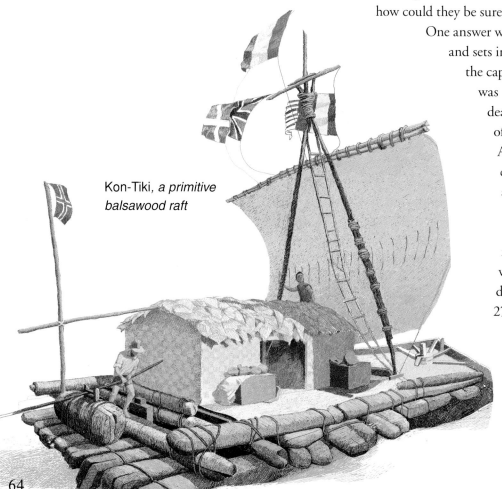

Kon-Tiki, *a primitive balsawood raft*

For decades, many people have wondered whether the islands of Polynesia (in the central and eastern Pacific) were settled by accident or by planned voyages of explorers. This quandary of human migration drove Norwegian ethnologist Thor Heyerdahl to undertake a fascinating journey on *Kon-Tiki,* a primitive balsawood raft. In 1947 Heyerdahl and his crew sailed a current, the South Pacific Eddy, for 101 days, traveling from the west coast of South America to a South Sea archipelago (chain of islands) of

of miles of the Pacific opposed to currents and winds. Whether ancient people *did* travel this way could only be guessed at. However, it certainly seems possible that centuries ago people may have had the navigational skills needed to partake in intentional exploration.

Polynesia. Their voyage demonstrated the possibility that the Polynesians originated in Peru, South America, 4,300 miles away! Unfortunately for Heyerdahl, scholars have accumulated much evidence over recent decades that has clearly refuted his idea.

In another bold attempt, sailors and researchers decided to test a hypothesis regarding ocean travel of ancient peoples from Hawaii to Polynesia. Their double-hulled Polynesian voyaging canoe, called *Hokule`a,* was built as closely as possible to what could be presumed from historical evidence. The craft set sail for Tahiti from Hawaii in May, 1976. In early June, the crew sighted Tahiti. Their journey proved only that this type of unique Polynesian canoe *could* cross thousands

Hokule`a, *a double-hulled voyaging canoe*

Chapter Ten

THE GENESIS FLOOD

Artist's depiction of ark interior

The world before the Genesis flood was very different from the world today. Christian author John C. Whitcomb suggested that it was a world "with its low-lying, fossil-free and ice-free mountains, its rainless sky and universally warm and humid climate, and its shallow seas." Upon this realm God sent worldwide judgment.

WHY DID GOD SEND THE FLOOD?

God hates sin and desires that all people should come to repentance. The conditions prior to the flood were those of extreme wickedness and moral depravity, not unlike today (Genesis 6:5-7,11-12; Romans 1:24-32). For example, there was a breakdown of the home and family (compare Genesis 6:2 and 2 Corinthians 6:14). It was also a world filled with violence (Genesis 6:11).

In Genesis 6:15, God told Noah, who had found grace in His sight (6:8), to build a floating barge 438 feet by 73 feet by 44 feet (a cubit in Scripture is about 18 inches long). These dimensions are similar to those of World War II aircraft carriers. The three-storied ark was able to hold the equivalent of 522 standard railroad stockcars of cargo. Just before the flood, God brought to this ark a female and male of all the earth's land animals. He also included seven pairs of the flying creatures, and seven pairs of clean animals, such as the lamb, which was probably to be used as part of ceremonial worship.

DID ALL OCEAN LIFE PERISH DURING THE FLOOD?

The phrase "all the fountains of the great deep [were] broken up" (Genesis 7:11) indicates that earthquake and volcanic action occurred on a global scale during the Flood. This geologic activity could have released tremendous amounts of juvenile water (water that was never part of the hydrological cycle) that was under pressure below the earth's crust. This source of water, plus the forty days and nights of rain, alone would provide enough water to cover even mountains (Genesis 7:20). All life on land and much ocean life perished during the year-long flood.

Evolutionary textbooks and museums show artistic displays of what scientists think life was like in the "Cambrian period, millions of years ago." What you really see in these large museum paintings is not the ancient "Cambrian period," but rather the buried remains of the pre-flood world. Creation scientists would say these colorful animals represent creatures that may have dwelt on the ocean floors before the Flood, a time period only thousands of years ago. The pre-Flood Earth was a place bountiful in the many types of unique and beautiful sea creatures that God created.

Today the oceans show only a portion of this incredible diversity, a large majority of those animals and plants having been destroyed by the devastating Flood. Remnants of pre-Flood life are now preserved as fossils to remind us of God's swift judgment on a world that was "filled with violence" (Genesis 6:11). These fossils include extensive deposits of fossil fish found in sedimentary strata throughout the world. In California, for example, fossil herring appear in the billions in the famous Monterey formation.

> "ON THE SAME DAY WERE ALL THE FOUNTAINS OF THE GREAT DEEP BROKEN UP . . . AND EVERY LIVING THING WAS DESTROYED" (GENESIS 7:11–23).

WERE THERE FRESHWATER FISH PRIOR TO THE FLOOD?

No one can describe exactly what the pre-Flood world was like. We have but two sources to consult: Scripture and the great sedimentary rock record found worldwide. Some fossil fish not only look like fish found in freshwater and brackish water today, but they are also found with fossilized algae and aquatic creatures found normally in those environments. This association suggests that fresh-water and brackish water fish, as well as marine (oceanic) fish, existed in the pre-flood world. Many of the freshwater fish that existed before the Flood undoubtedly perished.

WHAT HAPPENED TO FRESHWATER FISH?

Creation scientists cannot say for certain what the salt content was of the Genesis floodwaters. However, it can be speculated that the waters were slightly salty, although not as salty as found today. Despite the number of freshwater fish which perished due to the severity of the yearlong and world-wide Flood, some obviously survived the slightly salty waters to repopulate the freshwaters of the post-Flood world.

Saltwater and freshwater fish could have survived the Flood despite their temporary displacement. One way in which marine and freshwater fish could possibly have survived together was through the formation of a halocline, which is a strong density gradient. In other words, the huge freshwater outflow from the continents at the beginning of the Flood may have formed a stratification (density gradient) of shallower fresh water and deeper saltwater. This is known to happen currently on a smaller scale. Floodwaters flowing into the Gulf of Mexico during the great Mississippi flood of 1993 produced a layer of freshwater traceable all the way to the Florida Keys and the east coast.

Equally possible are marine fish surviving in the reduced-saltwater and slowly adapting to a purely freshwater existence as their offspring became land-locked centuries after the flood. This, of course, is not evolution as some would claim.

Perhaps these changes reveal a narrowing of the gene pool. Very adaptable fish of the past could have been affected by a loss, not a gain, of function. God has created virtually all life with an ability to adapt to environmental extremes, but still only reproducing "after its kind." A good example of this is the "cichlids," a fascinating fish kind that shows great diversity and adaptability. In the 1970s, biologist Arthur

Jones selected this fish as the subject of his doctoral research. He hypothesized that "all, or at least most, fish kinds that survived the flood must be able to survive both sea water and fresh, and much mixing of the two." His research revealed that his hypothesis was correct: some freshwater species not only survived over two years of living in a pure sea water environment, but they also "lived and reproduced normally."

WAS THE BIBLICAL FLOOD WORLDWIDE OR ONLY A LOCAL FLOOD?

A straightforward reading of Scripture would cause one to form the definite conviction that God was describing a world-wide event. Genesis 7:19 says, "And the waters prevailed exceedingly upon the earth; and all the high hills, that were under the whole heaven, were covered." Such language indicates what Bible students call an emphatic construction. In other words, He meant what He said! God clearly presents the Flood as being a worldwide catastrophe, not a local disaster. It is reasonable to believe that the mountains of the pre-Flood world were not as high as they are now and the floodwaters could easily cover them. Large mountain ranges seen today could have experienced a sudden upthrust. As one scientist stated, the "building of mountains still effectively evades an explanation." The great Colorado Plateau consists of hundreds of thousands of square

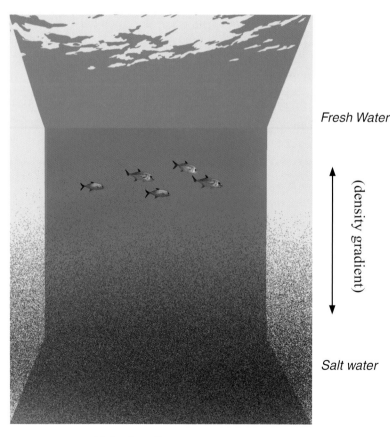

Fresh Water

(density gradient)

Salt water

Halocline diagram

miles of flat-lying sedimentary layers, each of which could have formed when under water, before the entire region was uplifted thousands of feet above sea level. Fossilized sea creatures are also found on the "roof of the world" — the towering Himalayas. Oceanographers and geologists admit that part of Mount Everest is made of rock made from sediments deposited "in a shallow sea" (or maybe deposited during the Flood?).

Practically all tribes and nations on Earth have retained some type of tradition or a variation of the account of the Flood at the beginning of their history.

Noah's ark was designed by God to withstand the ravages of this devastating Flood. The dimensions of the ark gave it the stability of a barge. It did not have to sail; it merely had to float. There was plenty of space for housing the various animals (including young dinosaurs!) during the 371-day stay aboard the ark. Noah and his family did not have to work "round the clock" to care for all these creatures because of the ability of some to fall into dormancy (hibernation). Feeding the non-hibernating animals did not require undue hardship on the crew because the animals were moving at a minimum and not expending a lot of energy. Specialized diets could have been provided for those few animals that required it.

Much physical evidence indicates a devastating flood as described in Genesis. A popular saying among flood geologists is "floods form fossils fast." Certainly the huge fossil graveyards made up of sedimentary rock — a large majority of which was laid down by water — are silent testimony of some rapid, cataclysmic event. The masses of vegetation that must have existed throughout the world prior to the Flood were covered by layers of mud, and, through heat and pressure, were carbonized into the great seams of coal found throughout the world today.

THE CATASTROPHIC FLOOD

The philosophy of uniformitarianism ("the present is the key to the past") has been used to guide the science of geology. This has since come under criticism because it simply assumes that the slow geologic processes seen happening today are the same as they have always been throughout the history of the world. Today, the better framework of catastrophism is replacing uniformitarianism.

Catastrophism means that, in the past, some catastrophic process or processes have changed the physical features of the earth. To use a familiar example, if a uniformitarian and catastrophist were looking at a house in ruins in the same way that they look at geologic evidence, the uniformitarian would assume that the house only fell apart due to age, weathering and insufficient repairs — decay factors that can be observed on a daily basis. The catastrophist would assume that a catastrophe like a hurricane or a tornado could have hastened or caused the house's decay. Some geologists insist that a look at the evidence reveals that practically every formation in the "geologic column" gives proof of being formed rapidly (e.g., massive underwater rock and mudslides called sediment gravity flows).

For years, geologists have been discussing superfloods that occurred in the past. Such events would be the kind of flooding that would be continental in scope. Other geologists speak of floods equal to a thousand Niagara Falls spilling across an area near Gibraltar "millions of years ago" refilling the Mediterranean Sea. Although they are not speaking of a worldwide flood, they certainly come close to the biblical account, based solely on their scientific observations!

A NUMBER OF SCRIPTURES LEAD TO THE CONCLUSION THAT THE GENESIS FLOOD WAS WORLDWIDE.

- The Lord Jesus believed in a worldwide Flood and compared it to the coming destruction of Earth when He returns (Luke 17:26-27 and Matthew 24:37-42).
- The purpose of the Flood was to destroy all mankind and animal life on the dry land not protected in the ark (Genesis 6:7; 7:22).
- The Flood was sent to destroy the earth (Genesis 6:13).
- The Flood covered all the mountains (Genesis 7:19, 20).
- The Flood lasted over a year (Genesis 7:11; 8:13).
- More than thirty statements of the universal character of the Flood and its effects occur in Genesis 6 through 9.

Submarine canyon

Underwater geologic processes can indeed be devastating. For example, November 18, 1929, an earthquake jarred sediments off Newfoundland that then funneled through canyons near the continental slope to the ocean floor. Loosened into a sediment gravity flow, the sediments slid down the slope close to an incredible 60 miles (97 km) per hour. The muddy slurry roared along the bottom, breaking twelve transatlantic telephone cables in such a way that the speed the sediments traveled could be easily determined. The last cable to be broken was 300 miles (483 km) away from the quake's center. The enormous sediment gravity flow lost energy in the deep abyssal plain after covering hundreds of square miles in just a few hours. We can contemplate that up to one-half of the North American continent was formed by such massive underwater avalanches. Processes such as this could explain the formation of continental rises, flat abyssal plains, and submarine canyons.

Even the fact that very well-preserved fossils occur on a worldwide scale indicates cataclysmic water action in the past. Recent research in the Redwall limestone of the Grand Canyon by creation geologist Dr. Steve Austin reveals an enormous kill zone of fossilized nautiloids. The deposit covers over 6,000 square miles (15,533 square km), and the billions of nautiloids are oriented (turned) to indicate the flow of a current such as one would find with a huge sediment gravity flow.

Engineers have measured the devastating power of waves and have found that typically they have more than 6,000 pounds (3 tons) of force per square foot. Imagine the earth-changing power of waves during a worldwide flood.

In 2002, science writer Paul Recer wrote a news story of "water roaring out of an overfilled lake [that] carved an instant Grand Canyon — a valley more than [a] mile (1.6 kilometers) deep . . . ." This is interesting because some flood geologists feel that this was the very process that formed the Grand Canyon in Arizona some time after the Genesis flood. Mr. Recer, however, was not writing about Arizona; he was writing about the planet Mars! He went on to say that this Martian flood "was enough to carve a valley 6,900 feet (2,070 m) deep and 550 miles (885 km) long within a matter of months. . . . " These dimensions are very close to those of Arizona's Grand Canyon. If it can happen on Mars, where no liquid water has ever been seen, certainly it can happen on Earth, whose surface is 72 percent water! So, contrary to what evolutionists state, it does not have to take a little water (such as in the Colorado River) to slowly form the Grand Canyon over "millions of years." A lot of water can do the same thing in just a few weeks or months.

MOUNT ST. HELENS

A 1982 eruption of Mount St. Helens in Washington — a world-changing catastrophic event that scientists actually observed — formed the majority of a 1/40 "scale model" of the Grand Canyon in just one day. The original eruption in May 1980 enabled flood

Mount St. Helens eruption

geologists to see what an enormous amount of energy can do on a local scale and helped them appreciate the intensity of a worldwide cataclysm. The 1980 explosion involved a rapid flow of mud and glacial water from the mountaintop causing destruction in a short period of time. As Dr. Steve Austin stated, "Mount St. Helens teaches us that the stratified layers commonly characterizing geological formations can form very rapidly by flow processes." In other words, it does not take "millions of years" to produce individual layers of sedimentary rock. Mount St. Helens showed that layered stacks of materials up to 600 feet thick (183 m) can be rapidly laid down.

Almost half of the sediments deposited on the continents are interpreted as marine deposits because they contain marine fossils and sediments caused by ocean invasion onto the land. A good example of one layer would be a widespread sand bed called the St. Peter sandstone, a million and a half square miles in area, up to 300 feet thick. This deposit of sediments contains evidence of the rapid movement of deep water. Geologists call the St. Peter sandstone a high-energy deposit; it covers a large portion of the United States. What kind of water activity would produce widespread flooding and depositing of sandstone on such a large scale? Only an equally extensive flood!

The end of the Genesis flood most likely came about by the sudden uplift of continents and mountain ranges and the corresponding deepening of ocean basins. The submarine canyons and seamounts in the world's oceans show evidence of such former lower levels. A writer in one encyclopedia described that evidence in this way: "Great changes in sea level of much more recent geological age are indicated by recent work. Great canyons, comparable in shape and extent to the Grand Canyon, cut through the continental slope. Again 'seamounts,' thousands of feet below the present sea level, have tops covered with large rounded boulders. In the present state of our knowledge it is difficult to see how these and other formations can have evolved unless these formations were at one time thousands of feet higher with reference to sea level."

All the world's great mountain ranges show evidence of earlier higher water levels. These evidences found the world over give a clear picture of a world in the process of emerging from a recent global cataclysm.

"The Sea is His and He made it"

The mighty, mysterious oceans are composed of pounding surf, frigid depths, pulsing tides, beautiful atolls, and creatures that provide us with food and entertain us with their bizarre features. This great liquid expanse composed primarily of two basic elements — hydrogen and oxygen — is as yet not known anywhere else in this immeasurable universe. Life on Earth depends upon the oceans which God, the Master Designer, has wonderfully created. We can agree with the cry of the Psalmist when he exclaimed, "the sea is his, and he made it" (Psalm 95:5).

> "THY WAY IS IN THE SEA, AND THY PATH IN THE GREAT WATERS, AND THY FOOTSTEPS ARE NOT KNOWN."
> – PSALM 77:19

Appendixes

OCEANIC EXPLORERS

CHRISTOPHER COLUMBUS (c. 1451-1506)

A Genoese sailor employed by the Spanish. A master mariner, he was determined to reach India by sailing west. In April 1492, his three fast, light ships with ninety men and a year's worth of provisions reached an island in the Bahamas. In March 1493, Columbus returned to Spain where Queen Isabella and King Ferdinand proclaimed him Viceroy of the Indies and Admiral of the Ocean Sea. Later that year, he set sail with seventeen ships and discovered Puerto Rico. In 1498 on his third voyage, after discovering an island with three mountain peaks close together which he named Trinidad (Holy Trinity), Columbus encountered Venezuela. He also discovered Cuba, Haiti, and other West Indian islands.

FERDINAND MAGELLAN (c. 1480-1521)

Portuguese navigator and world voyager, whose five-vessel expedition left Spain in 1519 (he was denied funds by his native Portugal). Magellan was the leader of the first expedition to circumnavigate the world. A strait at the southern tip of South America bears his name, due to his discovery of it in 1520. The rest of the voyage was not without a great price. Only 18 of his 270 sailors survived the three-year voyage. Magellan himself was killed by natives in the Philippine Islands. His men decided to continue sailing west, arriving back in Spain September of 1522. The voyage further opened the doors to the Americas as a New World to explore.

GERARDUS MERCATOR (Gerhard Kremer) (1512-1594)

Flemish geographer and mathematician. He surveyed Flanders and made terrestrial and celestial globes, becoming the leading mapmaker of the 1500s. He was the first to call a book of maps an "atlas." The Mercator map projection (1569) that bears his name is a cylindrical map projection of the features of the surface of the earth that can be constructed only mathematically. It was found to be ideal for ocean navigation and is still used today as sailors are guided by straight lines on flat charts instead of lines curved on globes. In 1585 he began a great atlas that was later finished by his son. His last years were given to theological studies.

Louis-Antoine de Bougainville (1729-1811)

An admiral and navigator from France. In 1766 he was sent by his government to make a voyage around the world (circumnavigation) taking from 1766 to 1769. He rediscovered the Solomon Islands in 1768, the largest of which is named for him. He also collected plants and made reliable charts of some areas of the central Pacific. Bougainville saw a portion of the Great Barrier Reef, but failed to discover Australia.

James Cook (1728-1779)

Cook conducted three South Pacific voyages of discovery that resulted in a number of accomplishments, including providing valuable charts and maps of New Guinea and the Pacific Coast of North America. In January 1778, while on his third voyage, he became the first European to reach Hawaii, then called the Sandwich Islands. Cook charted and explored many islands and atolls. He was also an accomplished scientist. Along with other naturalists aboard the *Resolution*, he took samples of animals and land plants, marine life, geologic formations and the ocean floor. Detailed descriptions were recorded in journals and logbooks. Unfortunately, while on his third voyage, Cook was killed by Hawaiian natives.

CONVERSION CHARTS

Mile	Nautical Miles	Fathoms	Feet	Kilometers
1	0.868	880	5,280	1.609
2	1.700	1,760	10,560	3.218
3	2.600	2,640	15,840	4.829
4	3.500	3,520	21,120	6.438
5	4.300	4,400	26,400	8.047
6	5.200	5,280	31,680	9.656

Meters	Feet	Fathoms
50	164	27
100	328	55
300	984	164
500	1,640	273
1,000	3,281	547
2,000	6,562	1,093
6,000	19,685	3,281

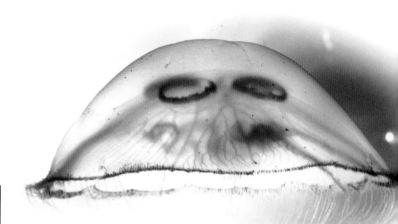

Feet	Meters	Fathoms
6	2	1
50	15	8
100	30	16
300	91	50
500	152	83
1,000	305	166
2,000	609	333
6,000	1,829	1,000

League	Miles	Nautical Miles	Fathoms	Feet	Kilometers
1	3	2.6	2,640	15,840	4.828
2	6	5.2	5,280	31,680	9.656
3	9	7.8	7,920	47,520	14.484
10	30	26.0	26,400	158,400	48.280

Nautical Mile	Miles	Feet	Kilometers
1	1.15	6,076	1.852
3	3.45	18,228	5.556
5	5.75	30,380	9.260

Bibliography

Austin, Steven A. Personal communication, February 5, 2004.

Berrill, N.J. *The Living Tide.* New York: Dodd, Mead & Company, 1951, p. 228.

Clark, William. *The Essential Lewis and Clark.* Edited by Landon Y. Jones. New York: The Ecco Press, 2000, p. 135.

Corfield, Richard. *The Silent Landscape: The Scientific Voyage of HMS Challenger.* Washington, DC: Joseph Henry Press, 2003, p. 52.

Eardley, Armand J. "The Cause of Mountain Building: An Enigma." *American Scientist* 45, June 1957, p. 189.

Jones, Arthur. *In Six Days.* Edited by John Ashton. Green Forest, AR: Master Books, 2001, p. 241-245.

Marinatos, Spyridon. "Thera: Key to the Riddle of Minos." *National Geographic*, May 1972, p. 715.

Morris, Henry M. and John C. Whitcomb. *The Genesis Flood.* Phillipsburg, NJ: P&R Publishing, 1961.

Recer, Paul (Associated Press). "Flood on Mars Carved Instant Grand Canyon, Researchers Say." *San Diego Union Tribune,* June 20, 2002.

Thompson, Ernest F. "Oceanography." *The Encyclopedia Americana*, International Edition, 1976.

Vago, R., E. Gill, and J.C. Collingwood. "Laser Measurements of Coral Growth." *Nature* 386, March 6, 1977, p. 30–31.

Whitcomb, John C. *The World That Perished: An Introduction to Biblical Catastrophism.* Revised edition. Grand Rapids, MI: Baker Book House, 1988, p. 46.

Illustration/Photo credits

Glossary

Abyssal — A term used for animals, water, or land in the deepest part of the ocean, 13,000 feet (4,000 m) or deeper.

Bathyscaph — A deep-diving submersible designed like a blimp. Its name means "deep ship."

Benthic — A term used for the ocean floor or animals living on or near it.

Brackish — Fresh water diluted with seawater.

Catastrophism — The philosophy about the past, which allows for totally different processes and/or different process rates, scales, and intensities than those operating today. Includes the idea that processes such as creation and dynamic global flooding have shaped the entire planet.

Centripetal acceleration — The force on a moving object that pulls it in toward the center.

Cephalopod — The group of animals containing octopus, squid, cuttlefish, devilfish and nautilus. This name literally means "head foot" and was probably given because these animals use their head to move.

Circumnavigation — To make a voyage around the world.

Convection — The transfer of heat by the circulation of moving currents in either air or water.

Crest — The highest part of a wave.

Diatomaceous earth — Sedimentary rock consisting mainly of fossilized diatoms, a type of algae.

Dorsal — The back or upper surface of an animal.

Drag — Friction created between the bottom of an advancing wave and the surface over which it is moving. Near the shore, this friction causes the wave's bottom to advance slower than its crest. Because of this, the wave topples, creating surf.

Ecosystem — The relationship between plants, animals and their surroundings.

Equatorial — Pertaining to areas near or on the equator.

Exoskeleton — The hard outer covering of many invertebrates. It provides support, protection, or both.

Fossil record — Animals, plants, and their traces solidified in sedimentary rock.

Gyre — Large oceanic currents found in each of the major oceans. Their movement is determined by flow of warm surface water toward the poles, the Coriolis force, and global winds.

Halocline — A rapid change of salinity with water depth. The saltier water becomes, the more dense (heavy) it will be. Less dense water (water with less salt) will sit on top of denser water unless mixed by currents or water movement. Coastal areas form haloclines where fresh water runoff flows over saltier ocean water.

Hydraulics — The branch of physical science involving the behavior of liquids in motion and at rest.

Hydroelectricity — Using water movement to produce electrical energy.

Hydrological cycle — The cycling of water between the seas, the atmosphere, and the land by evaporation, condensation, precipitation and other processes.

Hypothermia — A condition of significantly lower body temperature caused by exposure to cold.

Invertebrates — Animals without backbones.

Meteorologists — Scientists who study weather and climate.

Photosynthesis — Chlorophyll in green plants absorbs light energy which is then used to convert carbon dioxide and water into simple sugars. The sugar compounds store the energy needed to sustain both plant and animal life. Oxygen is released as a byproduct of the process.

Photosynthetic algae — One type of microscopic algae, called zooxanthellae, live in the layer of cells lining the stomach cavity of coral polyps. The carbon they provide through photosynthesis is used for both coral growth and respiration.

Plankton — Microscopic plants and animals drifting or swimming in the ocean waters.

Polyps — A single coral animal. Many polyps make up a colony of coral. The hard surface of a coral reef is made of calcium carbonate secreted by polyps in the colonies making up the reef.

Quadrature — When the sun, earth and moon form a 90-degree angle.

SCUBA — The military acronym for Self-Contained Underwater Breathing Apparatus or gear used when diving under water.

Sea mounts — Mountains on the seafloor that have pointed peaks and are at least 3,280 feet (1 kilometer) high.

Sediment gravity flow — Suspension or slurry of sediment mixed with water that moves solely due to gravity, typically thought to occur on deep ocean floors.

Sonar — The military acronym for sound navigation ranging, or echolocation.

Swell — When a pebble is dropped into a pond, the small waves formed move away until they meet the pond's edge or lose their energy. Swells are giant ocean ripples formed by storm winds or other disturbances, which have enough energy to move away from the influence of the disturbance. After traveling often long distances, swells can create high surf when they run into a coast.

Syzygy — When the sun and the moon line up with the earth in a straight line.

Temperate zones — The middle latitudes between the equator and the poles. This would be between 23½ to 66½ degrees latitude in both the north and south hemisphere.

Uniformitarianism — The philosophy about the past which assumes no past events of a different nature than those possible today, and/or operating at rates, scales and intensities far greater than those operating today. The slogan "the present is the key to the past" characterizes this idea.

Vertebrates — Animals with a backbone.

Index

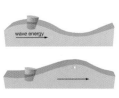

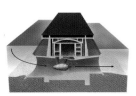